the green witch at home

the green witch at home

a guide to house magic for an enchanted life

cerridwen greenleaf

author of the best-selling *book of kitchen witchery*

CICO BOOKS

LONDON NEW YORK

With life's increasing pace, a magical approach to living is more important than ever. I bestow upon you these special spells, blessings, recipes, and rituals, handed down through generations of my family and friends. I also owe much gratitude to my teachers, Z Budapest and Starhawk, who showed me how to stay grounded with our Mother Earth and be always connected to spirit. Blessed be!

This edition published in 2022 by CICO Books
an imprint of Ryland Peters & Small Ltd
20–21 Jockey's Fields   341 E 116th St
London WC1R 4BW   New York, NY 10029

www.rylandpeters.com

10 9 8 7 6 5 4 3 2 1

First published in 2018 as *The Magical Home*

Text © Brenda Knight 2018
Design and illustration © CICO Books 2018

Editor: Rosie Fairhead
Designer: Mark Latter
Illustrator: Rosie Scott

Commissioning editor: Kristine Pidkameny
Senior editor: Carmel Edmonds
Art director: Sally Powell
Production controller: Mai-Ling Collyer
Publishing manager: Penny Craig
Publisher: Cindy Richards

A CIP catalog record for this book is available from the Library of Congress and the British Library.

ISBN: 978-1-80065-167-8

Printed in China

MIX
Paper from responsible sources
FSC® C106563

Contents

Introduction
Where the Heart Is

Your home should feel like a sanctuary. You should be able to walk in the front door and immediately feel comfortable—that you are in a place of refuge, a safe haven. At a certain point some months ago, my home no longer felt like a sacred space; I had stopped really "seeing" what was in my own sanctuary and allowed in a lower vibration. When I realized this, I looked at how I could make a change. By investing time in maintaining my home, I reaped many rewards—and you can do the same. This book offers a plethora of suggestions for things you can do, both large and small, to make a tangible difference to the way your home feels and functions, and to enhance your enjoyment of it. The ideas, spells, recipes, charms, and witchy feng shui tips in this book will go a long way toward fulfilling your bliss quotient.

You'll discover how to maximize good energy in your home by keeping it clean in an eco- and budget-friendly way, and how to transform it into a home spa with recipes for enchanting beauty products. Learn, too, how to nurture your relationships, both with a partner and yourself—simply caring a little more for your sleeping space can do wonders! When it comes to the kitchen, I'm a huge advocate of growing your own produce, and have offered my advice and tips on creating a bountiful garden, as well as recipes for your fruit and vegetables, and spells to imbue them with magical intent.

There will always be surprises, and that is part of what makes house magic so exciting. For example, I recently discovered that Virgo New Moons are a power phase for me,

despite being the opposite of my natal moon sign. If you keep notes on your magical workings in your Book of Shadows (see page 17), you'll discover what ideas, spells, and timings work well for you—especially when you begin to design your own rituals. You'll find out which phases and signs of the moon are optimal for you and your spellcasting, which herbs and essential oils are most healing for you and your loved ones, and which crystals and gemstones bring the most security and serenity to your home.

In focusing your attention on your home, you'll discover what might be holding you back from being utterly happy there, and you'll be able to use this wisdom to conjure pure contentment. I hope that this book offers all you need so that every time you come home, you'll immediately feel a sense of blissful coziness.

CHAPTER 1

Magical House Makeover

Secrets and Spells for Your Sacred Space

Do you come home every night and feel guilty about the piles of clutter? Is something blocking your creativity or your enthusiasm for household projects? Does your energy feel "stuck" in certain rooms, even so far as to impede a good night's sleep in your own bed? Aside from stopping you from having a peaceful and orderly home, a messy muddle and stacks of stuff can be an energy block, which can get in the way of the manifestation of prosperity and prevent abundance from entering your life. Pagans had their own kind of feng shui way before this became a fashionable trend. These witchy decluttering tips and rituals will help you to make your home a sanctuary once more, and a welcome bonus will be that your life will feel calmer, clearer, and more organized.

Divine decluttering

Getting rid of anything you no longer use will increase the functionality of your home by making it easier to clean; it will also increase orderliness and improve the energy. You should only have possessions that you really love; don't let your things possess you.

Recently, I made a breakthrough discovery when I decided to unpack boxes I had never opened since moving home six years earlier. Although they were tucked away unseen in the basement, I knew they were there. One New Moon in Virgo, I decided to take the plunge and open them. Going through our things can be an emotional experience: I found a card from a friend who had since passed away and immediately became misty-eyed. Powered by the efficiency of the Virgo Moon, however, I plowed through the boxes and placed objects in three designated areas: Donate, Trash, and Keep. The goal was to have as little in the "Keep" zone as possible. I am proud to say that even less was in "Trash," and that zone contained only items that broke during the move. "Donate" became several carloads to the recycling and reuse center. Once I got the knack of it, most of "Keep" ended up there, too. After the whirl of activity, something unexpected happened: I suddenly felt very buoyant, much lighter. It was then that I realized those unopened boxes had caused an invisible cloud of guilt; they had weighed me down. When the cloud lifted, I experienced a kind of effervescent joy.

Now I keep a neat-looking "outbox" on my front porch, and I fill it with items that I can take to the Reuse Center at my neighborhood recycling facility. As the days go by, magazines, extra pots and pans, odd cups and dishes, old electronics, and anything else that no longer has a place in my home goes into the box. My partner and I go to the recycling center at least twice a month, and it simply feels wonderful. I have seen amazing trades at the Reuse Center; I also witnessed a musician sit down and play a free sitar with virtuosity, while a family with young children got a sorely needed washing machine and dryer. Moments like this remind me of the visionary pagan teacher and writer Starhawk and her novel *The Fifth Sacred Thing* (1993), depicting a future in which people return to a barter system and live harmoniously in communities.

Take only what you need, and share anything extra with your own neighbors.

Clear a space and make it yours

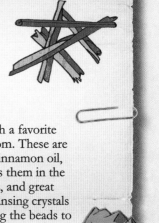

To clear and purify your space with as much of your own personal energy as possible, perform a ritual sweeping with a favorite broom or "besom." I use a sweet-smelling cinnamon broom. These are actually made of pine straw, coated with divine-smelling cinnamon oil, and set aside to dry for 3 weeks. Many a grocery store sells them in the fall and holiday season. The smaller ones make lovely gifts, and great altar adornments (see page 30). I ornament mine with cleansing crystals by stringing a colored silk cord with quartz beads, or gluing the beads to the base of the broom handle.

gems and crystals for space-clearing and purification

- **Amber** for positivity and happiness

- **Blue lace agate** for serenity and a peaceful home

- **Coral** for well-being and good cheer

- **Jet** to absorb bad energy from your environment

- **Onyx** as a guardian stone and protector

- **Petrified wood** for tranquillity and a sense of security

- **Clear quartz** for peace of mind and space-clearing

- **Tiger's eye** to protect from "psychic vampires" (energy-draining situations or people)

- **Turquoise** to create calm and facilitate relaxation

Clearing energetic clutter

Before you can do any ritual work, you must clear the clutter that can create blocks. Banish old, bad energy from your house by following this spell. First, make an energy-clearing lavender-and-mint tea by drawing fresh water, boiling it, and adding 4 sprigs each of fresh lavender and fresh mint (if you have no access to the fresh herbs, use 1 tsp of each dried herb instead). Steep for at least 4 minutes, and as long as 10 minutes if there is a lot of energetic clutter. Leave it to cool, then dip your finger in the tea and sprinkle it throughout your home while reciting:

Clean and clear, nothing negative near.

Only healing and helpful energies here.

With harm to none. So mote it be.

Repeat three times, and if you feel the need to clear out any remaining cloud of psychic clutter, add the diluted tea to your cleaner when you wash floors or surfaces. The scent of calm and clarity will lift the spirits of all who enter your space.

Herbal clutter busters

The purpose of incense is to release energy into the ritual space, and to clear the mind in preparation for the spell work to follow. It is not intended simply to create billows of smoke that can cause respiratory problems in the circle, so if you or someone else finds incense smoke irritating or worrisome, consider using another symbol of air instead, such as potpourri, fresh flowers, feathers, or a fan.

There exists an abundance of incense burners nowadays, so choose one that pleases you. Perhaps a smoking dragon or a goddess to hold the fiery embers of your incense would add to the energy of your altar.

Sweetgrass: For centuries, Native Americans have burned braided sheaves of sweetgrass, a hardy aromatic herb that grows in the northern hemisphere. It is so beautifully scented that it can also be wafted around unlit as a wand to clear energy. Native peoples also brew it into a tea to use as an astringent rinse for body and hair; you can do this by steeping 1 tbsp of the dried chopped sweetgrass for 5 minutes in a standard teakettle or 4 cups (900 ml) boiling water. It is also used as an adornment, woven into braids or as a crown. Native Americans believe that "strong hair means a strong mind." This powerful herb cleanses body, soul, and home, but the highest use is for rituals, when you can burn it to call forth the ancestors and send away anything unwanted.

Copal: Mexican and South American tribal healers and modern shamans gather the resin of the copal tree to use as ceremonial incense throughout the year. You will still smell the sweet, pungent smoke of copal in communities that celebrate the Day of the Dead, as it helps us to connect with our ancestors and loved ones who have passed to the other side. Burning copal is part of the ritual, but shamans and healers believe that it also helps to tap and cross over into the spiritual realm. Copal also has the power to bring total relaxation.

Palo santo: This dried wood from a tree native to Central and South America plays an important role in South American cultures, where it is burned to clear a space of bad energy. It also activates a higher power in those who use it. Its scent clears out psychic clutter and purifies both you and your environment. It is said that it can literally burn away negative thoughts in your mind— a deeply powerful experience.

Clearing the decks for health and wealth

Prosperity and purification go hand in hand. One of the greatest tools for purification is sage, and, while every metaphysical store has it in quantity, I highly recommend gathering or growing it yourself. Aromatic sage dries quickly and can be bound into thick "smudge sticks," which you should keep at the ready in a fireproof clay dish. To make a smudge stick, bind dried sage leaves into bundles with green and gold thread wound nine times around and knotted at each loop. Leave room for a handle at the base of the wand, where you wind and knot the green and gold threads thrice more. This will honor the Three Fates, who hold the thread of our destiny in their hands: Clotho, who spins the thread of life; Lachesis, who chooses its length and outcome; and Atropos, who cuts the thread.

Use your smudge stick any time purification is in order, especially if you've moved home, started a new job, bought a new car, or purchased any second-hand clothing or furniture. This will help to remove any energy that might be clinging from the previous owner or incumbent. If you have just performed a big decluttering in your home or office, you can further cleanse your personal space by smudging it with sage smoke.

Light your smudge stick and, moving clockwise, circle the area or objects to be purified. Speak these words aloud:

Great Spirit goddess so wise,
with this smoke,

your blessed protection I invoke.

Out with the bad, in with the good.

Harm to none and blessings to all.

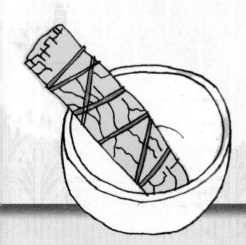

Change your life with sacred stones

It is useful to give a lot of thought to the constructive changes that you wish to see in your life, or the positive qualities that you want to develop further in yourself. Crystals and sacred stones can be a great source of clarity, and can help to process emotions. For example, if you want to become more organized, look out for lazulite. Of course, getting organized requires some letting go and getting rid of belongings that have seen better days. This used to be a real problem for me, as any of my friends can tell you, and my cozy cottage is lined with magazines, journals, and books, books, books! But, I really felt the need to declutter my life and streamline it—to become a bit more Zen. So, I had to get organized with lazulite power and then let go with lepidolite!

I have never really had any jade but, recently, I've felt the grounding and stabilizing effects of this stone are what I need. I must also become more prosperity-minded. I need to be better about saving money and thinking in terms of my future security, so I'm not reading tarot cards out on the sidewalk when I'm 90! For this reason I've been walking through San Francisco's Chinatown and feeling very attracted to different jades.

I'm sure you feel such urges and attractions, too. This might be your subconscious giving you a gentle nudge about some growing you need to do. Listen to those inner voices, and you will reap the benefits again and again.

the effects of sacred stones

- *Amber* for grounding
- *Aventurine* for creative visualization
- *Bloodstone* for abundance and prosperity
- *Carnelian* for opening doors for you and your family
- *Citrine* for motivation and for attracting money and success
- *Geode* for enduring periods of extreme difficulty
- *Hematite* for strength and courage
- *Jade,* a harbinger of purity and tranquillity, to help you simplify your home and life
- *Jasper* for stability
- *Lazulite* for decluttering, clearing away blocks, and helping to organize your mind
- *Lepidolite* (which should be called the letting-go stone) to help you get rid of old habits
- *Rhodochrosite* for staying on course with your life's true purpose
- *Watermelon tourmaline* for help with planning your best possible future

Ritual for letting go

- small table
- white candle
- copal incense
- white dish
- sage leaf
- small sheet of white paper
- black pen

Many of us have hoarded to some extent. I joke to my friends and family that I have "paper issues" with all my books and magazines, but I also amass colored glass vases and bottles, interesting chairs, quirky candleholders, and much more. I eventually realized that things had gotten out of control. When I really looked at my home, I knew I needed to give away a lot of things I didn't really even see anymore. It's hard, though, because we often want to cling onto possessions that have an emotional attachment even if we have not used them for years. Less really is more, though! The following spell for letting go will transform both you and your home.

First, set up a temporary altar by taking a few of the items you are giving away or selling, placing them on the table, and putting the table near the front door.

Light the candle and the incense, and intone:

As I walk in wisdom, this I know.

Material goods are meant to flow.

I rid myself of blocks so I can grow.

With this rite, I am letting go!

And so it is.

Take each item and record it on the sheet of paper. For example, write "Purple dish, with grace and gratitude, I let you go!"

After you have recorded all the items, read your list aloud. Then, carefully light the piece of paper and burn it in the white dish with the sage leaf while repeating the spell above. When the paper has burned to ash, snuff the candle and allow the ashes to cool down completely. Take the dish outside and toss the ashes into the air. Now go back in, pack up the newly released items, and get them out of your house, into the trunk of your car, a storage shed, or the nearest Goodwill or recycling/reuse center. Or try my idea of an outbox on the front porch (see page 10). The important thing is to get all those things out of your house so the energy flow inside is improved. If you moved bigger pieces such as shelves or chairs, I highly recommend a ritual floor wash (see page 40). Once you have done that, the energy in your home will shimmer and sparkle with freshness!

Pendulum divination

If you are having a hard time donating or getting rid of some of your belongings, or simply can't decide and find yourself surrounded by piles of confusion, pick up a pendulum. You do know what to do on an unconscious level, so pendulum divination is a way of gleaning information from your deepest self. I can't recommend it highly enough. Most New Age stores now sell pendulums on delicate chains, although some of the best pendulums are those you can make yourself by tying a piece of string or rawhide to a pebble, crystal, or coin. You should tie it so that the weight points downward.

Get in a comfortable position where you can lean your elbow on a table or flat surface, holding your arm steady with no movement. Let the pendulum swing freely until it comes to a rest. Now test it by first asking a question that you know is a yes, such as, "Is my name Cerridwen?" The direction in which it begins swinging will be the "yes" direction. Do the same for a question that you know to be answered with "no." Each time you use the pendulum, ask, "Show me yes or show me no." The pendulum will swing, giving you answers. I recommend keeping a journal of your work with the pendulum in your Book of Shadows (see below); pendulums do vary, so spend time getting to know yours and you will have a wonderful tool to turn to for life's questions. Not only will this give you a record of yes-and-no responses, but also it will help you to track their effectiveness. Soon, you'll be able to see patterns of information emerging from your unconscious and the universe.

You will learn a great deal about yourself and your place in the world from this. I know people who absolutely depend on their pendulums for help with shopping and all manner of decision-making. It is fun and full of surprises!

the book of shadows

Your Book of Shadows is your magical journal, a ledger for all your rituals, energy work, circles, spells, and all the magic you have manifested. It is a living document that you can apply to magical workings to come, and it will even help you to design your own spells and rituals. Use it to record the times and details of everything you undertake, so that you can see what works best for you. It is a book you will turn to again and again, so it should be very appealing to you. It can be a gorgeous, one-of-a-kind volume or a simple three-ring binder—choose whatever you find most useful.

Sanctuary spells and witchy feng shui

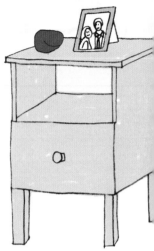

We all want the kind of home that feels, to quote our fairy-tale friend Goldilocks, "Just right." You can have that: It's not so much a matter of housekeeping as about "energy maintenance," since old, stale, or negative vibrations can linger in much the same way that dust clings to surfaces and must be wiped away. The following witchy feng shui tips will improve every area of your life. Applying what you learn as you go can be a marvelous way to ensure that your home will be a veritable enchanted cottage where you can live happily ever after.

feng shui secrets for peace of mind

Stones left in strategic places around your home can help to accelerate the change you desire. Using what I call "crystal feng shui," you can place a crystal or a geode in a particular position in your home to bring about specific results. Here are a few stone placements to try:

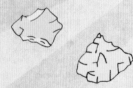

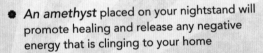

- *An amethyst* placed on your nightstand will promote healing and release any negative energy that is clinging to your home

- *Clusters of jade or yellow "lemon quartz"* on your desk or workspace will activate vibrations of abundance and creativity

- *A big chunk of citrine* placed on the left-hand side of your desk will bring more money into your home or office

- *An obsidian ball* can absorb negative energy—try putting it in a dark hallway that feels spooky, or any area where the energy seems very static or low

- *Rose quartz* can be placed anywhere in your bedroom to make it a place of bliss and unconditional love

Wind chime feng shui

By this point, you have made good progress in decluttering your home both physically and spiritually. It is now time to make kind and generous energies and benevolent spirits feel "at home." Make a wind chime of "shiny objects" such as old keys, bits of jewelry, and other items from your decluttering. For example, I have a lot of "mateless" earrings, which I love even though they are only one of a pair. These chimes gather the good energy of those unseen that can help to protect you and drive away the less helpful energy. Tie string around your shiny objects and attach them to a tree branch or stick (a small piece of sea-smoothed driftwood is perfect). I recommend using seven objects, because seven is a sacred lucky number, and I make sure they are close enough to touch one another and make that lovely, welcoming sound. Hang the chimes where they can tinkle gently in the breeze and make contact with your guardian angels for you—ideally in a window in your home or wherever you want to make contact with the spirit world.

To welcome the spirits, bless the new chime by smudging it with incense and sage smoke. Jingle the chimes energetically while you speak this spell:

*I call upon my angels
to guide joy to my door.*

*Such gladness as I receive,
so I shall give.*

By the moon and the stars

I call upon my guardians

To show me the best way to live.

*For this, I am grateful.
Blessed be.*

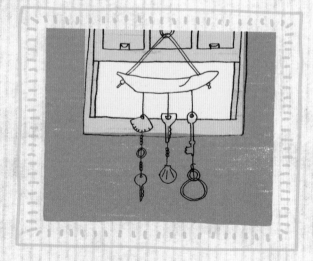

The scent of happiness

The minute you walk into someone's home, you can tell how happy a household it is. Much of that is determined by the smell. A home with the fragrance of sugar cookies or a freshly baked pumpkin pie is one you will want to visit often. Similarly, a space redolent of lilies or tea roses is obviously one whose occupants take care to make their home beautiful to the eye and the other senses. There are lots of small things that we can do in terms of "energy maintenance" for our home. This recipe works wonders on you or anyone in your environment who might need a lift.

- ❖ 2 drops neroli oil
- ❖ 4 drops bergamot oil
- ❖ 4 drops lavender oil
- ❖ 2 drops rosemary oil

- ❖ 2 pints (1.2 liters) distilled water
- ❖ spray bottle

Combine the essential oils, then add the mixture to the distilled water in a spray bottle. Spray the air while chanting:

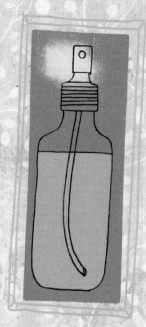

Gloom and doom begone.

Bright energies abound!

Welcome, sweet spirits, into this house.

With harm to none. So mote it be.

Western winds of change rite

This is the ideal mixture of essences to purify your home, your altar, or your sacred working space. Negative energy is vanquished and the path is cleared for ritual. It is also advisable to use this incense to clear any arguments or other energetic disruptions from your home. After a family squabble or, goddess forbid, a break-in or some other incident that makes your office, home, or temple space feel violated or less safe than usual, dispel the bad with this holy incense.

Crumble the dried sage and mix together with the other ingredients. Burn the mixture in an incense burner or censer. Open windows and doors when you are burning this incense, so that the "bad energy" can escape.

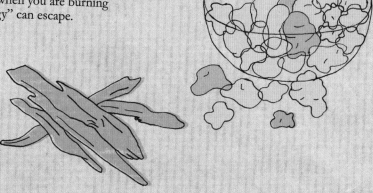

- 1 part dried sage
- 1 part sandalwood powder
- 3 parts myrrh resin
- 3 parts copal resin
- 3 parts frankincense resin

ghostbusting potion

To rid a house of haunting intrusion, brew a peppermint-and-clove infusion. Draw fresh water and boil it in your teakettle. Place three cloves in the bottom of a teacup and add either a peppermint teabag or a handful of fresh mint leaves from your herb pots. Pour hot water into the cup and let it steep for 10 minutes, then let cool. Dip your fingers in the cup and sprinkle the potion throughout the space, and out, out, the ghost will race. Burning frankincense and myrrh incense sends negative spirits flying away, as well. This ritual is best done during a waning moon (see Chapter Seven).

Privacy magic

Does the gentleman over the back fence seem too interested in your conversations? Do you have nosy neighbors or a nightmare roommate? Combat other people's lack of respect for your personal space and home boundaries with crystals. Jet (a type of lignite) is a gemstone formed under extreme pressure underground from wood. It is such a powerful energy cleanser that it can be used to cleanse your other crystals. When you have problems with the folks next door, place jet at your door or bury it by the fence. Soon, your nosy neighbor will find no need to linger by the fence and you will have reclaimed your privacy. If you have an intrusive roommate or guest, place jet on the mantel or bookshelf and wear jet jewelry to take back your personal space. Use this spell anytime you need protection from "space invaders." It is a wonderfully respectful and peacekeeping way to honor your need for solitude, and it harms no one. Nosy people are often lonely, so, when the time is right, offer a cup of tea and a chat and you will doubtless be rewarded tenfold for your largesse. Kindness is a very powerful magic.

Backyard blessings

As the saying goes, happiness can sometimes be found in your own backyard. To create a sense of serenity and peace, take a walk around your neighborhood. As you go, gather seven leaves from trees you see along your path, a handful of pebbles, and a fallen tree branch. Return to your home through the front door, looking at everything as if you were a visitor. Stroll into your backyard or garden. With the tree branch, draw a circle on the ground and mark four directions: North, East, South, and West. Place the stones and leaves at the center of the circle. Concentrate on your connection to the earth and how to honor that in your life. Incant this spell:

Good luck rises for me in the East;

My music rises in the South;

My wishes rise in the West;

From the North,
my dreams will come true.

Welcome home purification ritual

Over time, you will doubtless adorn your sacred space with many beautiful objects. I have restrained myself lately in keeping with my renewed dedication to decluttering, but there was a time when I could not pass up a small goddess statue. I still love looking at them, and they grace every room of my home. Whenever you acquire something new, you must cleanse it. Each item used in this ritual relates to one of the four elements.

❖ incense, such as cinnamon, which is wonderful for a happy home
  ❖ white candle
  ❖ cup of water
  ❖ small bowl of salt

Pass your possession through the scented smoke of the incense and say:

Inspired with the breath of air.

Pass it swiftly over the flame of the candle and say:

Burnished by fire.

Sprinkle it with water and say:

Purified by water.

Dip it into the bowl of salt and say:

Empowered by the earth.

Hold your new possession in front of you with both hands and imagine an enveloping, warm white light purifying it. Now say:

Steeped in spirit and bright with light.

Place the newly cleansed object on your altar and say:

By craft made and by craft charged and changed,

This use for the purpose of good in this world.

In the realm of the gods and goddesses,

I hereby consecrate this now.

Blessings to all, blessed be.

Room by room
Charms for a charmed life

Transform all your living areas with these simple spells and ideas. Making just small changes and additions can make a huge difference to the atmosphere in your home, so it is well worth taking the time on it.

Hallway
Salt lamp spell

Your entryway is where things cross the threshold into your realm, and energy management should start right at the front door. One way to keep constant vigilance on this is by having a Himalayan salt lamp in your front room. Salt is one of Mother Nature's greatest protectors, as it cleanses your environment of ill omens and bad spirits. When warm, these lovely blocks of rosy-hued salt produce negative ions—the very thing that makes a day by the ocean so cheering. A simple DIY way to have your negative ions and enjoy them, too, is to buy a batch of rock-salt chunks at your nearby New Age store or even a gourmet store. Making sure you are near an electrical socket, place a small string of white lights, such as mini Christmas lights, or a small wired light bulb in a metal or wire bowl. Gently pile the rock salt over the bulb, plug it in, and switch it on. The rock-salt crystals will glow soft pink, like the early-morning sun, and, as the rocks warm up, your mood will begin to lift. As a double benefit, the salt will constantly cleanse the energy in your home and keep it light and bright.

To consecrate your new energy-management center, hold one of the rocks and speak this spell:

I hold this salt, beauty of the green earth and the ocean.

I hold this wish for a happy and peaceful home to come soon.

May all be merry and bright far and near.

May all find contentment who enter here. Blessed be!

Adorn every door
Wonderful wreaths

A herbal wreath hanging on a door can be a source of love and luck. Wreaths on the main door of your house give protection to the home and send messages about the life within, or you can make wreaths for specific rooms—such as a wreath of healing herbs for the kitchen, the heart of many homes. Woody herbs, such as rosemary, are best if you plan to keep your wreath up for more than a day or two because they last longer.

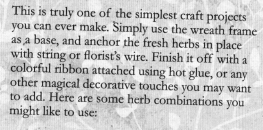

- ❖ wire wreath frame (available from most craft stores)
- ❖ freshly cut herbs of your choice
- ❖ string or florist's wire
- ❖ ribbon
- ❖ hot glue gun

This is truly one of the simplest craft projects you can ever make. Simply use the wreath frame as a base, and anchor the fresh herbs in place with string or florist's wire. Finish it off with a colorful ribbon attached using hot glue, or any other magical decorative touches you may want to add. Here are some herb combinations you might like to use:

Healing Wreath: The ideal herbs for a wreath that brings curative properties include lavender, barley, comfrey, rosemary, peppermint, borage, olive, eucalyptus, and apple blossom. Brown and green ribbons add a touch of healing color.

Protection Wreath: For a guardian wreath to hang on your front door, use heather, holly, dill, foxglove, garlic, sandalwood, snapdragon, mustard, foxglove, mistletoe, and mugwort. White and blue ribbons add security and serenity.

Abundance Wreath: Greet prosperity at the door with herbs associated with money magic: clover, chamomile, sunflower, apple, cinnamon, myrtle, basil, and bay. Weave in gold and green ribbon to add to your luck.

Love Wreath: Don't wait until Valentine's Day to try this—love should be 24/7. Invite it into your home by hanging a wreath full of love herbs on your door. Any combination of these will work beautifully, and I recommend using herbs that resonate for you personally from these options: allspice, clove, catnip, fig, bleeding heart, periwinkle, tulip, peppermint, violet, daffodil, lavender, and marjoram. Adorn your wreath with pink and red ribbons to let the universe know you're ready to welcome love into your life.

Living room Homemade pillows

Your living room, family room, or parlor is where you entertain and gather with loved ones to relax. It is essential to create a space where everyone can unwind and just enjoy life. A fantastic way to do that is to lovingly hand-make pillows that are cozy and filled with charm in every sense of the word. Choose fabrics in happy hues such as yellow, orange, or red, and smooth materials, such as silk or softest cotton.

Square pillows are very easy to sew, thanks to the simple, straight seams. I prefer hand-sewing, as it is very meditative. Simply take two pieces of cloth at least 12 inches (30 cm) square, lay them on top of each other inside out (that is, with the sides you want showing against each other), and pin them. Sew three of the seams and securely tie off the thread to prevent fraying. Turn the pillow right side out and tuck the pillow stuffing in. Carefully stitch the last seam to complete. Of course, you can also buy pillows and beautiful slip-on pillow covers.

For that extra touch of magic, tucking in tiny pouches of dried herbs that abet affection, such as chamomile or lemon balm, will greatly add to the conviviality.

Office
Knock on wood for luck!

When the economy starts to slide, secure your income and recession-proof your job with petrified wood. Petrified wood is actually a fossil formed from organic wood that has crystallized into quartz. It is rarer than rock crystal, so a small piece will provide plenty of magic. This security stone will be your bulwark when the sands of the marketplace begin to shift. As a bonus, it can make you physically stronger. Keep it on your desk and touch it when you feel worried; you will immediately feel calmer and more grounded.

Dining room
Candled crystals

I made candles as a young girl, and that hobby has now grown into a full-blown obsession. A few years ago, it occurred to me that I could make "stained-glass" candles by mixing big crystal chunks into the wax in the mold. An even easier way to do this is to stud the top and sides of a soft beeswax pillar candle with crystal pieces that cost just pennies per pound from New Age stores. I save them from the melted candles and use them again and again!

Stained-glass spell

Recently, I have been wishing and hoping for peace in this world of ours—as have most of us, I am sure. I have been making, burning, and giving away candles with the word "peace" written with crystals embedded in the soft wax.

If possible, perform this spell during a full-moon night for the greatest effect (see Chapter Seven). Place a stained-glass peace candle on your altar and light some rose incense, which represents love and unity. Light the candle and chant:

I light this candle for hope.

I light this candle for love.

I light this candle for unity.

I light this candle for the good of all the world.

That we should live in peace. And so it shall be.

Sit in front of your altar, close your eyes, and meditate for a few minutes while visualizing peace in the world. Let the candle burn down completely for the full magical effect.

Bathroom Scrying mirrors

Nearly every bathroom has a mirror over the sink, but you can add a touch of magic to yours. Round, oval, or rectangular mirrors are the best shapes for a magic mirror from which you can glean wisdom about the future.

❖ small mirror in your chosen shape (available at craft stores)

❖ soft, dry cloth

❖ clear-drying glue

❖ beads, crystals, shells, sea glass, or other decorations of your choice

Clean the mirror and its frame with a cloth and apply the glue to the front of the frame. Affix your decorations to the frame, one at a time, in any pattern you like.

To use your magic mirror, light candles and meditate in silence. Ask any questions you may have, and gaze into the glass. The answer may come into your mind, or an image might even flicker across the surface of the mirror. Record what transpires in your Book of Shadows. Different kinds of questing and querying may call for several different magic mirrors.

Painting your mirror

You can equally paint your mirror to personalize it. Some crafty witches I have known have decorated mirrors with concentric circles of color, following the spectrum from dark red to sky blue to grassy green, in gorgeous spirals and paisley prints all across the frame.

You could try the following colors:

● **Blue** for self-image and personal matters

● **Red** for matters relating to love

● **Green** for money matters

Bedroom Spell in a box

Native Americans, Greeks, Celts, and Egyptians all used magical boxes during ceremonies and for storing sacred objects. Christian religions followed suit: The famous biblical Ark of the Covenant was, in fact, a magical box. Such boxes can be made of wood, metal, marble, glass, cardboard, fabric, or whatever suits your need, and you can ornament yours as you see fit. In medieval times, spell work involved boxes for love, health, fertility at home and in the fields, prosperity, and changing luck. More recently, a young woman's "hope chest" might contain wishes, intentions, and materials for a happy marriage. These days it is just as likely to reflect hopes for a successful career, good health, and the happiness of herself and her loved ones.

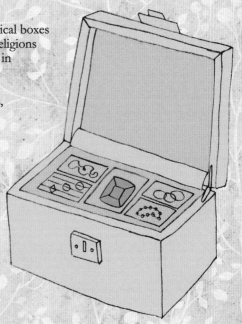

You can make charm boxes, also known as spell boxes, very easily. A job spell box should contain aventurine or peridot stones, patchouli incense, green candles, and ferns. You can make a psychic spell box with cloves, rosemary, and amethyst and quartz crystals. A good love spell box would contain a pink candle, rose petals, two pieces of rose quartz, and two copper pennies.

timing it well

It's a good idea to put your Book of Shadows to use for keeping track of moon phases and magical workings. Your results will show you which rituals were most successful, and when you carried them out. Remember the time you did an autumnal Pisces Full Moon ritual with your group and your home felt wonderfully fresh for weeks afterward? That is a strong indicator that this is an auspicious time for your spell work, which imbued your home with bright blessings. You will soon see a pattern emerging, and your ritual work will be all the stronger for it.

Altars

An altar is a physical point of focus for your rituals, and should contain a collection of symbolic objects that are assembled in a meaningful manner. Altars can be created for different purposes.

A house magic altar in your home provides a space where you honor the rhythms of the season and the rhythms of your own life and household (see below), or you can set up an altar for a specific purpose—for example, nurturing your relationship (see Pagan Feng Shui, Chapter 4). You can even make a nature altar—see pages 34–35.

House magic altar

Your house magic altar can be a low table, the top of a chest, or even a shelf. First, smudge the space with the smoke of a sage bundle or by burning sweetgrass or copal. Then cover the altar with your favorite fabric in a color you adore, and place a candle in each corner. I like to use candles of many colors to represent the rainbow array of gems. Place your chosen gems and crystals around the candles. Rose quartz is a heart stone, and fluorite is a calming crystal, so these are good options for grounding yourself, particularly if your altar is in your bedroom, as many are. Add fresh flowers, incense you simply love to smell, and any objects that have special meaning for you. Some people place lovely shells or feathers they have found on their paths or while at the beach, and others use imagery that is special—a goddess statue or a star shape, perhaps. The most important point is that your altar should be pleasing to your eye and your sensibilities. You should feel that it represents the deepest aspects of you as a person.

Ideally, bless your altar during a new moon. Light the candles and incense, and say aloud:

> Here burns happiness about me.
>
> Peace and harmony are in abundance.
>
> Here my happiness abounds.
>
> Gems and jewels—these bones of the earth
>
> Bring love, prosperity, health, and mirth.
>
> Be it ever thus that joy is the light
>
> That here burns bright. Blessed be!

You have now consecrated your altar. It will ease your spirit at any time, and become a source of power for you. It connects you to the earth, of which you and all gems and crystals are part, and it will connect you to the house magic that has now entered your life. The more you use it, the more powerful your spells will be.

Blessing in a breath

Sit in a comfortable position in front of your home altar and meditate. Think about your blessings. What are you grateful for at this moment? There is a powerful magic in recognizing all that you possess. Breathe steadily and deeply, inhaling and exhaling slowly for 20 minutes. Then chant:

Great Goddess, giver of all the fruits of this earth,

Of all bounty, beauty, and well-being,

Bless all who give and receive these gifts.

I am made of sacred earth, purest water,

Sacred fire, and wildest wind.

Blessing upon me, Blessing upon thee,

Mother Earth and Sister Sky,

And so it is.

Oracle of Delphi Prophecy incense

This incense can bring on psychic dreams and will tell you what you need to know today, tomorrow, or 20 years from now.

❖ 2 parts rosemary sprigs
❖ 2 parts dried thyme
❖ 2 parts dried chamomile
❖ 1 part ground cinnamon
❖ 1 part lavender sprigs
❖ 6 drops peppermint oil
❖ 6 drops jasmine oil

To make the incense, put the herbs in a mortar and grind with a pestle. Transfer the crushed herbs to a glass bowl, add the essential oils, and mix together using a wooden spoon.

Place this prophetic pagan incense in a censer on your bedroom altar or on your nightstand and allow the scented smoke to imbue your sleeping space with its unique energy before you drift off. Prophetic dreams may come to you and—even better—you will remember them. If you are searching for specific answers, burn this incense for a whole week and record your findings in your Book of Shadows. Keep track of what you learn, and reflect on it. There is deep wisdom for you in the messages that come in your dreams.

Fireplace altars

Vesta is the Roman cognate of the revered Greek goddess Hestia, "first of all divinities to be invoked" in classical rituals. The ancient Greeks had public hearths called prytaneums (Prytaneions). These came under the domain of Hestia, protector of "all innermost things," according to the great philosopher Pythagoras, who also claimed that her altar fire was the center of the earth. The altar of Vesta in classical Rome was tended by the Vestal Virgins, and was also believed to be the very center of the earth. The insignia for the goddess was an altar table with flames at both ends, forming the Greek letter *pi*, which is the numerological symbol for the Pythagorean sect. We have come to know and love Vesta as the goddess of hearth and home.

The Vestal Virgins were the keepers of Rome's eternal flame. It was believed that if the fire of Vesta's altar went out, the Roman Empire would fall. In the late fourth century CE, with the rise of Christianity, the Vestal fire was extinguished and the process of erasing pagan religions and symbols began.

Fireplace altars today hark back to this earliest custom. Home and hearth have primal appeal to the comfort of both body and soul, and if you have a fireplace, it can become the hub of your home. The fireplace is also one of the safest places for ritual work involving fire. Sanctify your fireplace and altar tools, such as your bolline (magical curved knife), with a sprinkling of salt, while murmuring a prayer of thanks to Vesta. Like the Vestal Virgins of old, you can keep a fire burning in a votive glass holder in the back of your fireplace and have an eternal flame. The fireplace can be your simplest altar and a reflection of the work of nature. If yours doesn't contain a real fire, you can place sacred objects in it instead: pretty rocks, feathers, seashells, glistening crystals, beautiful leaves, and anything else that you feel represents the holiest aspects of the world around you. Let nature be your guide.

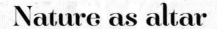

Nature as altar

To dispel negative energy and overcome any blocks you feel are keeping you "stuck" in your life, go for a walk in the nearest park. Find a round, flat rock 6–10 in. (15–25 cm) wide, bring it home, and clean it. I have also found landscaping rocks and paving stones at gardening stores that make marvelous outdoor altars, too. This will become an altar supplied directly to you by Mother Nature, and it will have the purest energy. Begin by charging the stone at your home altar during a full moon. Light a white candle for purification, then place your hand on the stone and chant three times:

Goddess of Night, moon of tonight,

Fill this stone with your light,

Imbue it with all your magic and might,

Surround it with your protective sight,

So mote it be. Thank you, dear Goddess.

Ideally, you'll want to perform this spell three times during three consecutive full moons before you begin drawing upon the energy of your altar stone. Like your home altar, your stone or nature altar will be a reservoir to which you can turn anytime you feel stuck or uninspired. Place it in your backyard or preferred outdoor space, perhaps a deck or balcony, and turn to it when you require rejuvenation. You can also specifically invoke Persephone, a goddess of spring (see page 128), by placing a pomegranate on your natural altar and adding her name as the first word of the spell given above. Make sure to thank any deity you invoke in your spell work.

sacred stone shapes for outdoor altars

- *Ankh-shaped stones* represent the key to life; develop creativity, wisdom, and fertility

- *Diamond-shaped stones* attract riches; bring the energy of wealth and abundance

- *Egg-shaped stones* give new ideas to the wearer; denote creativity

- *Heart-shaped stones* promote romance, self-love, and love energy

- *Stones with naturally formed holes* offer visions if you look through the hole by moonlight

- *Human body-shaped stones* bring energy and strength to whatever body part they resemble

- *Pyramid-shaped stones* bring energy upward

- *Rectangular rocks and crystals* contain the energy of God; symbolize male energy; offer protection and are good for love and sex spells

- *Round stones* symbolize the universe, the Goddess; spirituality, femininity, pregnancy; they are used in love spells to promote attraction

- *Square stones* bring prosperity and plenty; represent the earth

- *Triangular stones* are guardians and protect the wearer

CHAPTER 2

Magical Homekeeping

Making Your Own Organic Cleaners, "Green" Witchery Eco-detergents, and Non-toxic Paint

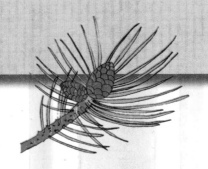

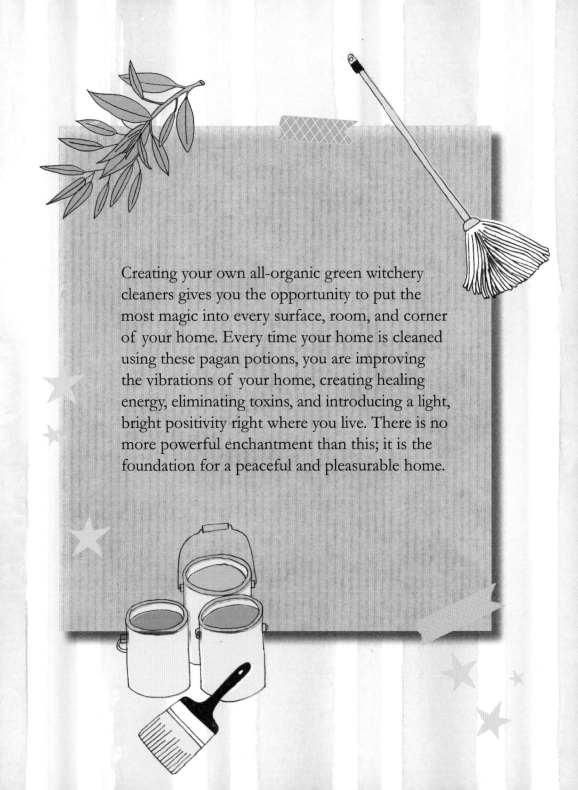

Creating your own all-organic green witchery cleaners gives you the opportunity to put the most magic into every surface, room, and corner of your home. Every time your home is cleaned using these pagan potions, you are improving the vibrations of your home, creating healing energy, eliminating toxins, and introducing a light, bright positivity right where you live. There is no more powerful enchantment than this; it is the foundation for a peaceful and pleasurable home.

Homemade organic cleaners

We all want to live in an enchanted cottage—a charming residence in every sense of the word. Several years ago, I learned that the chemicals in our cleaning products introduce toxins into our lives, along with a certain amount of negative energy. Who likes the smell of raw bleach, over-perfumed detergent, and those scary oven cleaners? They strip away the natural and are simply too harsh. It is even dangerous to have them around young children, whose curiosity could lead them into trouble. I think we can all agree that it makes sense to simply remove anything in the kitchen cabinet that is marked "poisonous." There are so many alternatives that are inexpensive and will make your home— and anyone who walks through the door—healthier and happier.

DIY all-purpose cottage cleaner

Baking soda (bicarbonate of soda) is miraculous for tough stains, rust, ovens, tiles, tough grease, smelly fridges, and many other household problems (but it is a mild abrasive, so don't use it on fine furniture or delicate fabrics).

Put all the ingredients in a bowl and mix well, then transfer to a clean spray bottle and shake.

For tougher-than-usual cleaning, add 1 cup (225 ml) white vinegar to the mix.

❖ 1 tsp baking soda (bicarbonate of soda)

❖ 1 tsp liquid Castile soap

❖ 3 drops lemon essential oil or 1 tsp lemon juice

❖ 2 pints (1.2 liters) warm water

Good housekeeping spell

Before special gatherings, or anytime you feel the need to do a deep cleaning on both the physical and spiritual plane, take your newly homemade eco cleanser while it is still in a bowl and place it on your altar. Light a white candle and speak this spell:

My home is a temple of love and light.

I now fill it with peace and beauty for tonight.

May all who enter this temple space

Bring laughter and joy and fill it with grace.

So mote it be.

Good-for-wood eco floor cleaner

Your floors will look great and smell even better with this floor cleaner that's specially designed for wooden surfaces.

Mix all the ingredients in a large glass bowl and pour into a clean spray bottle. Spray on the floor and wipe with a clean, damp mop. Follow by mopping with hot water. Allow the floor to dry a little and buff with a clean, dry cloth onto which you have sprinkled a few drops of lavender oil.

BE CAREFUL
Use caution even with homey, organic ingredients, and avoid getting vinegar, lemon juice, borax, or any of your eco witchery concoctions in your eyes.

❖ 1 tbsp white vinegar
❖ 1 tbsp olive oil
❖ 5 drops lemon essential oil
❖ 2 pints (1.2 liters) warm water

Floral floor cleanser

I haven't used store-bought cleaners since 2004, when a health challenge awakened me to the importance of ridding my environment of toxins and potentially harmful chemicals. I think it is a good idea for us all to consider doing this, since our health is precious, and I know this change made a difference to me and my loved ones. The smell of a home freshly cleaned with lemons and scented natural oils is wonderful. This is a magical floor wash for any purpose (although do leave out the lemon if your floor is delicate or made from antique wood).

- 1 cup (225 ml) hot water
- 3 sprigs mint
- ½ cup (110 ml) lemon juice (about 4 lemons)
- 8 drops lavender oil
- 3 sage leaves
- 3 cinnamon sticks
- 2 pints (1.2 liters) white vinegar

Pour the hot water into a large glass mixing bowl, and add the mint, lemon juice, lavender oil, sage leaves, and cinnamon sticks. Stir and let steep for a half hour.

Fill a clean bucket with 2 gallons (7.5 liters) warm water and the white vinegar. Using a kitchen strainer (sieve), strain the herbal mix into the bucket and stir with a wooden spoon. Dip a brand-new mop into the bucket, wring it out, and clean the floor thoroughly, speaking this spell as you work:

Spirits ill and energy dark, I cast you out!

Sadness, anger, illness, and doubt, I cast you out!

Welcome contentment and glee;
this home is now happy and free.

So mote it be.

Floor washes for money and love

You can use the basic vinegar, water, and lemon recipe and method for the Floral Floor Cleanser and add the following herbs and oils to produce the effect you want.

Buckets of money floor wash: To create abundance and bring money quickly into your household, add 1 cup (20 g) each peppermint and basil leaves and pine needles, 6 drops patchouli essential oil, and 6 drops bergamot essential oil.

Enchantment floor wash: If you are setting the stage for a new relationship, you'll want to scrub all the floors in your house, especially in and around the bedroom, living room, and anywhere else you are spending time with your romantic interest. Add 1 cup (20 g) sage leaves, 6 cinnamon sticks, 1 cup (20 g) pink or red rose petals, ½ cup (50 g) cloves, 1 cup (200 g) sliced apples, 6 drops rose essential oil, and 6 drops jasmine oil. Bonus tip: If you have any land around your home, use the strainer full of herbs as a "mulch" in the ground outside your bedroom, and the energy will integrate and protect your love energy.

Do-it-yourself homekeeping magic

As well as your wonderful All-purpose Cottage Cleaner, you will also need products that can help you take on more specific tasks. The following cleaners will be able to deal with anything that might come up in your home, and all are made from simple, easily available ingredients—some of them even quite surprising!

Scrub a dub

To make your own all-natural cleaning scrub, try this simple recipe: Mix ½ cup (140 g) baking soda (bicarbonate of soda) with ¼ cup (60 ml) liquid Castile soap to make a paste the consistency of frosting. Scrub any surface that needs cleaning, then rinse with water. Do bear in mind that baking soda is slightly abrasive, so fragile fabrics and surfaces—including glass, mirrors, and antique or rare woods—may not fare well. Do a little test, then, if no problems arise, scrub to your heart's content.

Eco laundry detergent

Want to get away from the chemicals, foaming agents, and synthetic fragrances found in most laundry detergents? This one will work beautifully in cold or warm cycles. Use a box grater to grate a bar of pure soap into a powder (it is easiest if you freeze the soap first), then mix the powder with 1 cup (140 g) borax, 1 cup (140 g) washing soda, and a few drops lemon juice (optional). Use 1 or 2 tablespoons of your detergent per load.

WORTH THE WORK

Eco cleaning solutions take a bit more effort, but are always worth it in the end. Not only are you saving money, but also you are making your home a healthier place for your family. Green is healthier and happier!

Tea tree wipes

Instead of the toxic, chemical-laden wipes you can buy at the store, make your own to keep handy for unexpected spills and scheduled cleanings. Mix 1 cup (225 ml) white vinegar, ½ cup (110 ml) lemon juice, and 8 drops tea tree oil. Soak clean cloths or paper towels (kitchen towels) in the mixture and store in a screw-top jar or resealable bag for wipes that last up to a month.

USE IT OR LOSE IT

Because they contain no preservatives, DIY cleaning mixes don't last very long, so use regularly for a clean green home!

Distilled vinegar

If I could clean my home with only one thing, it would be vinegar. A natural disinfectant that costs just pennies, vinegar deals with dirt, smells, stains, grease, and mold—especially in the shower. I've cleaned my whole house with just a spray bottle of vinegar and a little liquid soap. To make it smell really wonderful, add a few drops of calming lavender oil (also a natural disinfectant). Just remember, you're not making gallons, you're making a small bottle.

Blessed baking soda

Baking soda (bicarbonate of soda) is a wonderful deodorizer around the home, and can be used to freshen clothing, furniture, and carpets. It can also be used as an eco-friendly oven cleaner. When cleaning your oven—which is, after all, where you cook food for you and your family—it's better to skip chemicals, which leave an unhealthy residue. Make a paste by adding water, or equal parts water and vinegar, to 1 cup (140 g) baking soda. There will be a temporary foaming reaction so use a big bowl to avoid any mess and mix well. Use the paste to coat the inside of the oven and leave overnight. In the morning, turn the oven on low heat for an hour, then leave to cool. Use a spray bottle of equal parts water and vinegar to soften the hardened paste, and use elbow grease to scrub it off. When you are baking that next batch of cookies for your loved ones, you can rest assured that no fumes will get into the yummy treat!

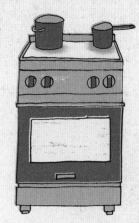

Yogurt: the pagan polish

Can you believe that your breakfast yogurt is also an effective cleaner for copper? Use plain yogurt to clean and polish copper pans, kitchen accessories, and basins. Most conventional alternatives contain a lot of chemicals. Coat the copper with plain yogurt, leave it until it turns green (about 30 minutes), then wipe it away with an old cloth. The copper will shine brilliantly.

Of course, use coarse salt

Some people swear by scouring pots, pans, and cooking surfaces with salt. It absorbs oil and grease, making it great for the stovetop, which can accumulate cooking splatters that are tough to remove. Sprinkle it on and scrub away with a damp sponge. Salt is magic!

secrets to stain removal

- If you spill coffee or red wine on your couch, carpet, or tablecloth, pour plain table salt into the spill immediately and it will soak it right up. The salt turning purple-blue as it soaks up red wine is truly spellbinding! Vacuum it up and the stain will be gone.

- Soak stained clothes, towels, and bed linens in cold water with baking soda (bicarbonate of soda) or white vinegar, and wash in cold water only to avoid "setting" the stain.

- There is no need to use bleach for white fabrics in your laundry: Use 1 cup (140 g) borax instead.

Lunar lemon power

Lemons contain the energy of the moon and the element of water. They can even be used to honor lunar deities. For millennia, people have used lemon oil in washing water for clothes and linens, or cleaned their homes using hot water containing lemon leaves.

The versatility of this beloved yellow fruit is fantastic. Instead of discarding lemon halves after you've used the juice for cooking or for making lemonade, save them to use around the home. This citrus fruit is a natural lightening agent that you can use in place of bleach (which should be used sparingly, if at all). And did you know that it can also perk up limp lettuce and kill weeds in the garden (see opposite)?

Uses in the home

Clean cheese graters: Cut a lemon in half and run it over the grater. The acid in the lemon will help to break down the fat in the cheese. If the food is really stuck on the grater, dip the lemon in table salt and the salt will act as a scrubber; combined with the lemon, it will remove most foods.

Sanitize metal jewelry: The acid in lemon juice also removes tarnish. Use just ¼ cup (60 ml) freshly squeezed lemon juice to 1½ cups (335 ml) water. You can also dip your silver into a glass of fizzy lemon soda (lemonade) and it will come out sparkling. But don't use this combination on gold or pearls.

Preserve meat and clean your cutting board: Lemon juice creates an acidic environment, and bacteria need an alkaline environment to survive, so adding lemon to meat, fresh produce, and even water inhibits bacterial growth. A handy antibacterial and natural way to clean your cutting board after cooking meat is to rub lemon juice on it and let it sit overnight, before rinsing it in the morning. The lemon juice will kill bacteria and leave your board smelling fresh.

Naturally restore furniture and wood floors: Mix equal parts mayonnaise, olive oil, and lemon juice, and rub into wood furniture. This mix will add oil to the wood, and the lemon juice will cut through any build-up of polish. For floors, mix a little fresh lemon juice with olive oil.

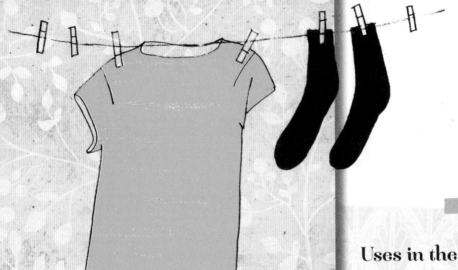

Brighten white tiles, sinks, and tubs: Mix fresh lemon juice with baking soda (bicarbonate of soda) and use to clean discolored ceramics before rinsing thoroughly.

Prevent rice from sticking: Add 1 tsp lemon juice to the pot while the water is boiling to keep the grains from sticking together and to enhance the whiteness of your rice. Other citrus fruit has the same effect.

Get rid of grease: Copper pots are cleaned quickly with half a lemon dipped in salt. Rub over a tarnished copper-bottom pot and you'll see magic; the same combination works really well for removing grease from a stovetop and from stainless-steel pots and pans. For a real build-up of grease, this method is your chemical-free solution.

Whiten your whites: Throw discolored white cotton socks, towels, or shirts in a stockpot with water and a few used lemons and simmer for a little while to lighten. (Only do this with pure cotton fabrics, and do not attempt this method with anything containing elastic.) If you hang them outside to dry, the combination of sun and your low-cost lemon whitener will refresh them until they are practically gleaming!

Uses in the garden

Kill weeds: Forget chemical weedkillers, which can be just as bad for you as they are for the planet. Control weeds with my lemon and white vinegar recipe, which is four parts lemon juice to one part white vinegar. Pour into a spray bottle, shake well, and head out into the garden, taking care to spray only the weeds. They will shrivel and die, making them easy to pull out and compost.

Deter pests: Lemon rinds placed around the border of your herb and flower garden will keep away pests, ranging from insects to pets and animals.

Natural home decorating

Most of us don't even realize that store-bought paints, varnishes, and latexes give off chemicals into the air you breathe. This is bad for our lungs, brain, skin, and everything else. There are so many toxins around us that reducing them in our personal environment is essential.

Gaia's green witchery flour paint

Flour paint is especially useful as a substitute for whitewash on outdoor walls, fences, and sheds. As you can tell from the ingredients, this paint contains few chemicals and is almost as natural as can be. Stop breathing in unnecessary toxins: Grab a brush and start beautifying!

❧ 2 cups (280 g) wheat flour

❧ 6 cups (1.35 liters) cold water

❧ 3 cups (675 ml) boiling water

❧ 1 cup (85 g) mica filler (available at any art or craft store)

❧ 1 cup (130 g) screened clay (available at any art or craft store)

❧ natural dye of your choice: tea, turmeric, berry juice, wine, or other organic colorant

Whisk the flour into a bowl containing 3 cups (675 ml) of the cold water. Pour the boiling water into a pan, add the flour mixture and simmer for 10 minutes. Mix well. Remove from the heat and add the remaining cold water. Let cool. Meanwhile, mix the mica filler and clay thoroughly in a separate bowl. Stir into the cooled flour paste, and add the dye.

Flour paint usually requires more than one coat, especially if it is used for indoor walls or furniture. Clean your brushes with warm water afterward. Allow two days for the paint to dry.

witch color magic

If you are going to paint your walls, fences, furniture, and she-sheds, you should be very careful in your choice of color. Every aspect of your spell craft can be enhanced using colors that amplify your intention. Here is a simple guide to color magic for you to explore:

- *Red* is for action, passion, vitality, strength, survival, fertility, courage, sexuality, conflict, independence, assertiveness, competition, and standing out

- *Orange* brings joy, creativity, expressiveness, intellect, the release of addiction, business success and ambition, vitality, fun, new ideas, and sociability

- *Yellow* is used for enjoyment, inspiration, success, happiness, learning, memory and concentration, persuasion, imagination, charm, confidence, and travel

- *Green* is for prosperity, abundance, money, physical and emotional healing, growth, luck, marriage, plant magic, acceptance, and counteracting envy and possessiveness

- *Light blue* represents spirituality, tranquillity, peace, protection, and growth

- *Blue* is used for communication, willpower, focus, forgiveness, good fortune, truth, patience, harmony at home, orderliness, removing bad vibrations, sincerity, and true-blue loyalty

- *Indigo* is ideal for spiritual guidance, mindfulness, psychic ability, divination, meditation, ambition, dignity, and overcoming depression

- *Violet* is the color of spirituality, connection to higher self, insight, clarity, tension, and the divine feminine

- *Lavender* is for aspiration, knowledge, and accessing intuition

- *Purple* is associated with wisdom, elders, influence, driving away evil, changing one's luck, independence, breaking habits, and spiritual power

- *Pink* is the color of love, compassion, nurturing, femininity, friendship, romance, partnership, spiritual and emotional healing, the protection of children, and personal inner work

- *Brown* is for house blessings, animal magic, material goods, stability, food, and forests

- *Gray* is best for contemplation, and for removing negativity in your environment

- *White* connotes newness, cleansing, purity, peace, balance, healing, truth, and spirituality

- *Black* stands for grounding, wisdom, learning, protection and security, reversing hexes, removing negative energy, transformation, defense, scrying, and secrets

- *Silver* is for feminine divinity, psychic awareness, intuition, dreams, victory, communication, luck, and moon magic

- *Gold* represents masculine divinity, great fortune, abundance, prosperity, understanding, divination, fast luck, positive attitude, justice, health, attraction, luxury, and magic involving the sun

- *Copper* brings business success, passion, money, fertility, and career growth

A magically clean home

Cleaning and decorating your home with products that are kind to the environment and your budget is a wonderful thing. You can also "clean" the energy of your home, too, by ensuring you have consecrated your new homemade cleaners (see below) and through rituals such as the New Moon, New Home ritual opposite. Energy maintenance is a key part of homekeeping, and having decluttered and improved the feng shui following the guidance in Chapter 1, it is important to ensure no negative energy creeps back in.

Love the earth eco cleaner consecration

I like to consecrate my homemade cleaners, since homekeeping is a sacred act, affecting everyone who lives in and visits your home. Going the extra mile to make your own eco cleaners is an act of love: You are helping to preserve the health of your friends, your family, and yourself. After you have mixed up your potion, chant aloud:

This potion I use in our home both above and below.

With each cleansing ritual, good health for all will rise and flow.

From Goddess Great comes all bounty, as we know.

With love in my heart, I will make this home glow.

Love Earth Now!

And so it is.

New moon, new home

The new moon is the best possible time to make big changes, start a new project, or do a deep clean and energetic shift of your home (see Chapter Seven). First, clean your home from top to bottom, and wash bed linen, towels, rugs, and tablecloths. Sweep and wash floors, recycle old newspapers, sort through those piles of paper on your desk, and get rid of things you don't need to keep; file everything else. Gather toys and games and put them in baskets for easy storage. Once your entire home is clean, decluttered, and lemony fresh, take the next step of the new moon ritual with a gathering of your fellow pagans. Ask each guest to bring food to share, and a small token to bless your home—crystals, flowers, seashells, candles, and other suitable altar offerings.

Greet your guests and ask them to help you by smudging each room with the salt, sage, candle flames, sprinkles of water, and incense, while intoning:

❖ saucer of sea salt

❖ sage for smudging

❖ 1 white candle and 1 blue candle

❖ blue bowl filled with fresh water

❖ lavender incense

❖ lemon essential oil

❖ rose essential oil

> *By the power of water,*
>
> *Through the cleansing breath of air,*
>
> *With the purifying heat of fire,*
>
> *And the grounding energy of earth*
>
> *We cleanse this space.*

As you pass from room to room, anoint each door and windowsill with the oil to prevent anything negative from crossing into the home. Say this prayer to the goddess:

> *May the goddess bless this house,*
>
> *making it sacred and safe,*
>
> *so that nothing but love and happiness*
>
> *shall enter through this door.*

Finally, once you've gone through the house, ask each guest to deposit their blessing token on your altar. Gather around the table, dig into the potluck dishes, and pour hearty glasses of ale, wine, or mead. Give thanks for the abundance of blessings and enjoy a feast with your tribe.

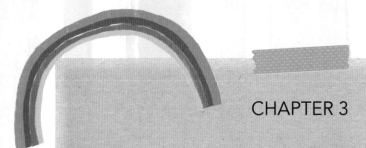

CHAPTER 3

Super-Natural Home Spa

Concocting Your Own Soaps, Lotions, and Potions for a Healthy, Happy Body

Self-care involves, in great part, living in harmony with the seasons and the natural world. Using a lot of chemicals in your home and personal care products goes against this, so take stock of what your soaps, shampoos, and cleansers contain, and do a detox. A plethora of organic options are available, particularly in health-food stores, and those redolent of natural essential oils will please both the eye and the nose. You can also make your own, so that every ingredient is under your control and you can customize for loved ones.

Does your mother love the scent of old-fashioned roses? Why not make her a batch of the Wonder Woman Body Whip on page 58 using some rose essential oil? If your best friend is always complimenting you on your vanilla scent, the sugar scrub on page 53 will make a perfect gift for her. The recipes in this chapter will bring you many compliments and, most important of all, make you feel wonderful.

Mother Nature's DIY beauty bar

The best beauty secrets are often hidden among our world's flora and fauna. Forget spending a fortune on overpriced creams, lotions, masks, and salves; simply head to the herb pots on your windowsill or check your pantry for organic remedies and common beauty solutions. Here are some of the best recipes and natural ingredients to help you begin your journey toward a healthy and non-toxic beauty regime. Always test your potions on a small area of your skin before using them more extensively or giving them to someone else; I use the pulse point at my wrist and wait at least half a day to check for any redness or irritation.

Yummy spa scrubs

Gentle abrasives in the form of body scrubs exfoliate and stimulate the skin—the body's largest organ—while helping it to stay nourished and moisturized. Massaging yourself with these is also good for the lymphatic system. It is extremely affordable and oh so easy to use what you already have on hand, such as sugar, baking soda (bicarbonate of soda), and coffee grounds. Binding substances—including oils such as almond oil, coconut oil, olive oil, and, my personal favorite, sesame oil—keep the abrasives together while you scrub. You can use honey to bind the mix, too, if you don't mind a little stickiness. Let your imagination run wild with extras such as added fragrance or decoration—spices, essential oils, or even flower petals. Keep glass jars with sealable lids handy so you can store your scrubs for up to two months. Add pretty labels and you have appealing and practical gifts for your coven of gal pals!

Here are four simple scrub combinations for you to try. For each one, simply stir the ingredients together in a bowl until well mixed (you may need more or less oil than specified), then decant into a glass jar. Be sure to rinse the bathtub or sink thoroughly after use to avoid stains or stickiness.

venus vanilla sugar scrub

- ❖ ¼ cup (45 g) brown sugar
- ❖ ¼ cup (45 g) white sugar
- ❖ about ¼ cup (60 ml) organic olive oil (to taste)
- ❖ 6–8 drops vanilla essential oil

VARIATION
You can vary this combination by using all brown sugar instead of a mix of brown and white, and trying other essential oils. My absolute favorite is equal parts vanilla oil and amber oil—I call it "vamber." It is great for when you're getting ready for a date or a night out on the town. You will look and feel like the goddess of love herself.

morning brew coffee scrub

- ❖ ½ cup (85 g) coffee grounds
- ❖ ½ cup (100 g) fine sea salt
- ❖ 1–2 tbsp almond oil

coconut colada sugar scrub

- ❖ 1 cup (85 g) brown sugar
- ❖ 3 tbsp melted coconut oil
- ❖ 1 tsp each ground cinnamon and ground cloves

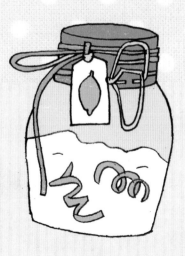

zesty lemon sugar scrub

- ❖ ½ cup (100 g) white sugar
- ❖ 2 tbsp lemon juice and 1 tsp lemon zest
- ❖ 1 tbsp olive oil

Mystical herbal mask

Warm oatmeal and chamomile tea conjure up a soothing feeling just at the thought of them—and they can also be an important part of your beauty regime.

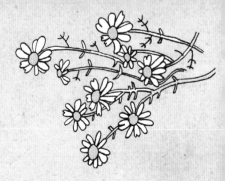

- ❖ up to 1 cup (225 ml) chamomile tea, steeped for a half hour
- ❖ 1 tbsp honey
- ❖ 1 tsp baking soda (bicarbonate of soda)
- ❖ ½ cup (50 g) old-fashioned oats, ideally steel cut, crushed using a fork or ricer
- ❖ 2 tbsp brown sugar

Put ½ cup (110 ml) chamomile tea in a small bowl and add the honey, baking soda (bicarbonate of soda), and oats. Add 2 tbsp more tea to create an oaty paste. Set aside for 5 minutes. If the mixture is too dry after this time, you can get the desired texture by adding a little more tea. Add the sugar and mix well. Apply the face mask to clean, damp skin. Allow it to dry for 10 minutes, then rinse off thoroughly and massage your face gently with a natural moisturizer. Your skin will be miraculously smooth!

Lemon meringue mask

This simple homemade mask tightens pores and leaves your skin feeling unbelievably fresh and renewed.

- ❖ 1 egg white
- ❖ 1 tsp freshly squeezed lemon juice

Beat the egg white with a whisk until it forms stiff peaks. Slowly stir in the lemon juice and whisk well to blend. Slather the mixture onto your face and neck. While the mask is drying, add the last ingredient, magic! Speak this spell:

With my hands, I made this;

With my soul, I bless this.

My heart is glad, my mind is clear.

With harm to none and health to all.

Blessed be.

When the mask has hardened, rinse it off thoroughly with warm water and enjoy your newly radiant skin.

Grapefruit almond joy lotion

Once known as "the forbidden fruit of Barbados," grapefruit awakens the mind and body, and speaks to the soul. Like many other citrus, it is cheering to the mood and renowned for what it does for skin —it can even reduce cellulite. Almond is beloved for bringing luck in romantic matters, and is prized as an erotic massage oil. Coconut protects, purifies, and enhances confidence; it brings forth your real allure and beauty, so use it carefully! This is a real treat: a creamy body lotion that glides on and does not feel heavy. With its delectable scent it will delight any of the gal pals on your gift list. A mixer is ideal for making it, but if you don't have one, use a hand whisk.

❖ 2 tbsp raw shea butter
(at room temperature)

❖ ½ cup (110 g) virgin coconut oil
(which is solid at room temperature)

❖ 2 cups (450 ml) almond oil

❖ 2 tbsp grapefruit zest

❖ 2 tsp tapioca flour

Place the shea butter, coconut oil, almond oil, and grapefruit zest in the bowl of a mixer fitted with the whisk attachment. Mix on medium power for 30 seconds, then turn to high and mix for about 4 minutes, until it is light and fluffy. Scrape the sides of the bowl as needed to make sure everything is combined. Add the tapioca flour and mix for 1 minute. Transfer to a jar with a lid. The lotion will keep at room temperature for up to a month.

OATMEAL SKIN SOOTHER
Naturally calming oatmeal is one of the best solutions for irritated and itchy skin, helping to return it to its normal smooth and healthy state. Add a cup of finely ground oats to the bathtub, tied up in a muslin bag, to soothe the pain and discomfort of sunburned skin. It is also good for rashes.

Love your hair homemade shampoo

There are many chemicals in haircare products, and they can contribute to early hair loss, so do detox your routine as much as possible. Don't start your days by coating your head in chemical compounds such as sodium lauryl sulfate and artificial fragrances, both of which can be toxic and are commonly found in shampoos and conditioners. By making your own haircare products, you will also avoid contributing to the problem of plastic waste. Witches are known for their Rapunzel-like locks, and with this organic approach, I predict people will stop you in the street to ask how you make your hair so beautiful! They will be astonished to know that you use just two simple ingredients each time you wash your hair.

❖ 1 cup (225 ml) warm water
❖ 1 tbsp baking soda (bicarbonate of soda)

Pour the water into a large bowl, add the baking soda (bicarbonate of soda), and stir well until it has dissolved. Now, pour over wet hair. Rub the mixture into your hair, paying special attention to massaging your scalp. If you tend to have oily hair, concentrate your efforts around the hairline and the crown of the head. If you have long hair, you can double the amounts. Rinse thoroughly and dry as normal.

Apple goddess hair conditioner

The goddess of the orchard is Pomona, a protector of nature, associated with love and beauty. You will be protecting your lovely locks by creating this simple yet effective DIY conditioner. It's remarkable how well these two ingredients work to clean and condition your hair. You will save a mind-boggling amount of money, and your hair and home will be healthier. Many people assume vinegar is irritating to the skin, but it's actually quite the opposite: It neutralizes pH and softens the skin, so it's great for irritated scalps.

❖ 1 cup (225 ml) warm water
❖ 2 tbsp apple cider vinegar

Mix the water and vinegar in a bowl and pour over freshly shampooed hair. Gently massage into your hair and scalp and leave for a few moments before rinsing. After a couple of months of DIY hair love, your tresses will be shockingly shiny. Place an apple on your altar and offer your thanks for the goddess Pomona for her generosity and guardianship of fruit orchards around the world.

Apple-a-day skin toner

This recipe also uses apple cider vinegar, which will become one of your best-loved beauty fixes and a household mainstay.

To make a skin-soothing facial toner, mix one part water and one part vinegar and wipe gently over a clean face using a cotton swab or soft clean cloth.

Blissful massage bars

Massage bars should look, smell, and feel luxurious. Cocoa butter is beloved for its delicious chocolate scent, but you could also use sumptuous shea butter or mango butter. Use your favorite essential oil to create a scent you will love.

Heat the beeswax, almond oil, and cocoa butter slowly in a bain-marie or double boiler over a low heat until just melted. Remove from the heat and let cool slightly. Stir in the essential oil. Pour the mix into the molds and let cool for about 2 hours, until hardened. Place in the freezer for a few minutes to make it easier to pop the bars out of the molds. To use, rub the massage bar onto the skin—the warmth of your body will immediately begin to melt the bar.

If you package your handmade soaps in a pretty box, they will make a wonderful gift.

❖ 3 oz. (80 g) beeswax
❖ ½ cup (120 ml) almond oil
❖ 3 oz. (80 g) cocoa butter
❖ 1 tsp essential oil
❖ soap bar molds
(available at craft stores)

Wonder woman body whip

Lather this decadent mixture all over your skin as you get into the bathtub, then ease down into the water and just soak. It is fabulously luxurious and will nourish your skin wonderfully.

❖ 1 cup (220 g) virgin coconut oil (which is solid at room temperature)

❖ 4 drops essential oil

Put the coconut oil in a medium-sized bowl. Using a hand mixer or an electric mixer with a whisk attachment, whip the oil until it reaches a soft consistency, like whipped cream. Add essential oil in a scent you love and whip to combine. Use every bit for your wonder woman treatment; you deserve it.

Mint miracle foot therapy

After a long day at the office, out hiking, or even dancing at your drum circle, your feet will be "dog tired." This pagan pick-me-up will soon have you out and about again, feeling fresh and fabulous.

Grind the mint leaves thoroughly into the coconut oil using a pestle and mortar. Transfer to a bowl, then stir in the vinegar and essential oil. Place the mix in the freezer for 5 minutes. Sit on the side of the bathtub and gently massage the mix into your feet, giving every toe and heel lots of loving attention. Take your time—your feet do a huge amount of work all day, every day. When you are satisfied, rinse your feet clean in the shower. Now, you deserve to put your feet up and just enjoy life for a while.

❖ handful of crushed mint leaves

❖ 3 tbsp solid coconut oil, warmed and softened

❖ 1 tsp white vinegar or apple cider vinegar

❖ 3 drops mint essential oil

Home spa rituals

A few years ago, a global study revealed Denmark to be the happiest country on Earth. Why are the Danes so joyful? One big reason is their love of home spas. However, there is no need to pack up and move to Scandinavia—you can enjoy the same relaxing and rejuvenating benefits in your own magical home with these rituals. You'll find inspired ideas and practical approaches for sacred self-care, which will definitely add to your happiness quotient!

Venus body blessing

This is a lovely ritual to indulge in before any special occasion, and you can also work it into your witchy calendar for an end-of-the-week rite of happiness. Fridays are ruled by Venus, so this is the perfect time for this body blessing. After a soak in the tub with the Venus Vanilla Sugar Scrub (see page 53), stand in front of your bedroom altar and anoint yourself with vanilla essential oil on your pulse points (throat, wrists, backs of knees) and over your heart. Hold your hand over your heart and say:

Goddess of the faraway star in the sky.

I ask you for health, youth, and wisdom to know why.

On this night, under your kind domain,

Please see that blessings of love, well-being, and joy remain.

Blessed be thee. Blessed be me.

Pagan potion blessings rite

Whenever you make a batch of salts, scrubs, or magic potions, whether for your own use or as a gift, stop and count your health blessings with this mindfulness practice.

Sit in a comfortable position with your newly filled bottle or jar in a bowl or dish in front of you. Think about the blessings in your life and the gifts your particular item offers. Visualize your skin and hair gleaming with vitality, for example, or picture your loved ones wearing a big smile as they use your handmade remedies. What are you grateful for at this moment? There is a powerful magic in recognizing all that you possess and in cultivating an attitude of gratitude. Breathe steadily and deeply, inhaling and exhaling slowly, for 20 minutes. As you meditate, send positive energy into the bowl. Now the blessings are there any time you or a loved one may need them.

Mother Earth gratitude chant

Fruit is wonderful to use in your supernatural spa treatments. It is also regarded as one of the purest forms of the earth's abundance. Whenever you make and enjoy these delightful recipes, show gratitude for these gifts from nature. Sprinkle thyme, flower petals, and ground cinnamon in your bathtub as you use these masks and scrubs. As you soak, say aloud:

Mother Earth, I thank you for the strength

and bounty of your earthly paradise.

Your beauty is reflected now and forever.

Forever grateful I will be.

Blessed be.

Your gratitude will be rewarded tenfold, and you will enjoy a shower of gifts in your life from Mother Nature, who enjoys getting credit for her good works.

 SUPER-NATURAL HOME SPA

Garden herb soak

We all get worn down by the sheer busyness of life. Oftentimes, when we feel depleted we get a little sad, too. To rid yourself of negative emotions, try this purification soak. Draw a warm bath at noon, when the sun is at its healing peak, and add 2 drops each of rosemary and peppermint oil and 3 drops each of lavender and thyme oil to the water as it flows from the faucet (tap).

As you soak and steam, repeat this prayer four times:

Sadness, I release you—goodbye.

Fatigue, I release you—goodbye.

I greet this day anew. My life is now renewed.

Blessed be me, so mote it be.

spa feng shui: sauna serenity

In Finland, people hang bunches of wonderfully fragrant silver birch branches near their saunas, and they use them to gently brush their skin to stimulate circulation. This sauna practice is deeply relaxing and can be a marvelous communal experience. You can emulate this by hanging herbs from your shower rod or above your bathtub. As the steam hits them, their aromatic oils will infuse the air.

I recommend bunches of lavender for tranquillity and eucalyptus to aid with colds and congestion. A muslin bag filled with dried orange rind, dressed with orange essential oil, will lift depression. Rosemary can help you to process sadness and grief, and activates your memory. A big bag of mint leaves is a major mood booster and sends concentration levels soaring. After a few uses, these herbs can be dried by laying them on a baking sheet and leaving in a cool, dry place for two weeks. Once dry, tie into a bundle with twine and use in a bonfire for the high holidays. Enjoy the holy and sweet-smelling smoke as it ascends to the heavens!

Self-expression spell A song for myself

Speaking of wonder women, you are pretty wonderful, too. This is definitely one of the more entertaining solo rituals. It requires you to look hard at yourself, but it's also fun.

❖ white candle

❖ peppermint essential oil

❖ spicy incense, such as cinnamon

❖ warm milk

❖ white mug

❖ sprig of fresh mint

❖ 2 cinnamon sticks

❖ large sheets of butcher paper (available in craft stores)

❖ colored pens

❖ decorative materials of your choice, such as glitter, beads, shells, cloth, ribbon, yarn, scraps of fabric, and buttons

It is good to undertake this ritual on a Sunday, but whenever you need support, reserve a half hour of quiet time and brew up some willpower to help you with your self-expression. Anoint the candle with the peppermint oil and light it; also light the incense. Pour warm milk into the mug and stir in the mint clockwise using the cinnamon sticks. Sip the drink to prepare for your Song of Myself, and recite the following words:

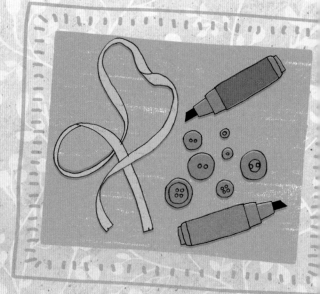

Herb of menthe and spicy mead.

Today is the day I will succeed

In every word and every deed.

Today I sing the song of me.

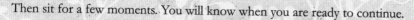

Then sit for a few moments. You will know when you are ready to continue.

Now take the paper and pens and begin your Song of Myself. Write with any color of pen you pick up and complete this sentence at least 24 times: I am _____.

Be as wild and free and true as you can. You are so many things. Express them here and now, once and for all. To inspire you, here are some wonderful "Songs of Self" that I have seen and heard:

I am a wild woman.
I am beautiful.
I am wide.
I am a secret.
I am sexy.
I am brilliant.
I am a blue sky.
I am all possibility.
I am a dream come to life.
I am truth.
I am the Goddess.
I am the living incarnation of wisdom.
I am life.

I am a living blessing.
I am the road.
I am perfect.
I am a tiger.
I am yesterday and today.
I am hope.
I am angry.
I am art.
I am a crone.
I am a sister to the sun.
I am a poem.
I am creative.
I am me!

This can go on for as long as you want it to. Only when you feel you have expressed every aspect of yourself should you put down your pens and begin to decorate the paper. Paint on it, glue mirror shards to it, make one or many self-portraits. Scrawl symbols on it, or write more words. Allow yourself absolute creative freedom. There is no wrong or right; there is only you and all your myriad aspects. Celebrate yourself and reveal yourself completely. By the end, you should have a one-of-a-kind self-portrait that tells your real story.

Hang your self-song portrait in a sacred place, perhaps near your altar area. Its energy will permeate the place with your personal essence in a wonderful way.

Crystal chakra healing

I have already suggested ways to use crystals in house magic (see pages 11, 15, and 18), but this healing practice is aimed at harnessing their power for you. It is distilled from the study of chakras. By working with your chakras, you can become much more in touch with your body and soul.

Healing stones

Here are just a few examples of how to apply stones directly to your body or that of anyone else who needs healing.

Lapis lazuli and its fellow blue crystal *aquamarine* can be laid on the throat chakra to release any blockage there. This greatly aids self-expression and is wonderful for professional speakers, as well as performers, such as actors and singers.

Turquoise laid on the face—cheeks, forehead, and chin—is a calming agent, significantly reducing tension.

Azurite on the brow opens the third eye and deepens wisdom; this can balance the energy of the head and allow more light into the third eye.

Malachite, a heart stone, placed near the heart and along the center of the abdomen will create a sense of harmony and help you to let go of pain, suffering, and childhood wounds.

The chakras

The root chakra is at the base of your spine, and is associated with passion, survival, and security, and the color red.

The sacral chakra lies above the root chakra, in the abdominal region, and corresponds to such physical urges as hunger and sexuality; its color is orange.

The solar plexus chakra is yellow and is associated with personal power.

The heart chakra is green (combining the soul color of yellow, and the spiritual color of blue) and symbolizes harmony, creativity, health, abundance, and nature.

The throat chakra is blue and is considered to be the center of communication.

The third-eye chakra is in the center of your forehead, and is associated with intuition and the color indigo.

The crown chakra, at the very top of your head, is your connection to the universe and is associated with violet.

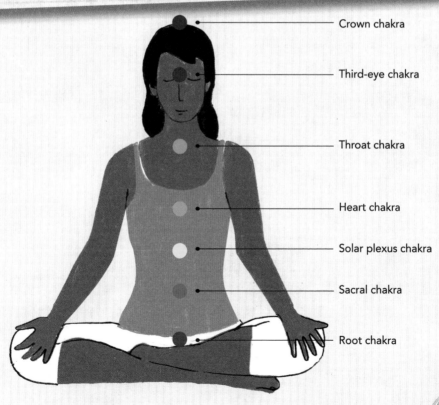

Crown chakra

Third-eye chakra

Throat chakra

Heart chakra

Solar plexus chakra

Sacral chakra

Root chakra

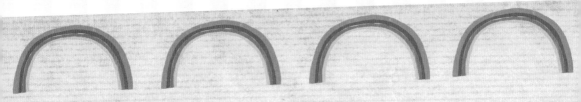

Rainbow renewal

The Rainbow is a simple and effective method for total-body wellness. For this healing practice, you will need seven stones, one for each color of the rainbow—violet, indigo, blue, green, yellow, orange, and red. Provided opposite is a list of crystals I would suggest using, including their body affinities in case there is a specific area you want to focus on.

The first step for anyone undertaking crystal healing is to lie down, relax, and get very comfortable. Empty your mind of all thoughts, and breathe deeply. Now place your chosen stones on their corresponding chakra centers. I recommend keeping the stones in place for a half hour, but I have seen positive effects take place in just minutes. While you are relaxing, visualize yourself enjoying total wellness, free of the malady you are treating.

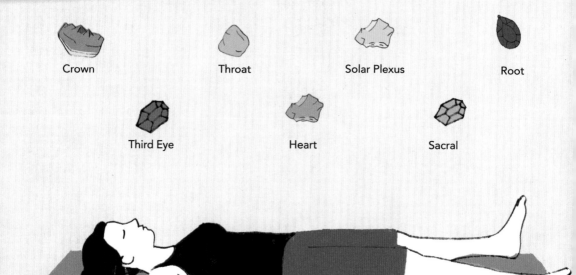

Crown

Throat

Solar Plexus

Root

Third Eye

Heart

Sacral

crystals and their body affinities

CROWN CHAKRA

- *Jadeite* for the knees
- *Dendrite agate* for the nervous system
- *Moonstone* for the womb
- *Purple fluorite* for the bone marrow
- *Amethyst* for sobriety

THIRD-EYE CHAKRA

- *Lapis lazuli* for the throat
- *Celestite* for the intestines
- *Calcite* for the skeletal system
- *Fluorite* for coordination and balance

THROAT CHAKRA

- *Blue tourmaline* for the thymus
- *Benitoite* for the pituitary
- *Lapis lazuli* for the throat
- *Dioptase* for the lungs
- *Celestite* for the intestines

HEART CHAKRA

- *Chrysocolla* for the pancreas
- *Chrysolite* for the appendix
- *Chrysoprase* for the prostate
- *Beryl* for the eyes
- *Moldavite* for the hands
- *Moss agate* for circulation and to boost the immune system

SOLAR PLEXUS CHAKRA

- *Calcite* for the skeletal system
- *Jasper* for the shins and for the skin
- *Danburite* for the muscles
- *Fluorite* for the teeth
- *Citrine* to protect the aura

SACRAL CHAKRA

- *Amber* for the thyroid
- *Fire agate* for the stomach
- *Coral* to calm and soothe nerves
- *Orange calcite* for the bladder
- *Chalcedony* for the spleen

ROOT CHAKRA

- *Bloodstone* for the kidneys
- *Carnelian* for the liver
- *Garnet* for the spine
- *Hematite* for the blood and circulatory system
- *Rose quartz* for the heart
- *Fire agate* for the stomach

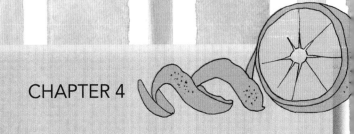

CHAPTER 4

Bedroom Magic

Charms, Spells, and Fabulous Feng Shui for Rest, Renewal, and Romance

Your bedroom can and should be a place of real enchantment. The spells and charms recommended for this most personal of spaces are those for love, health, relationships, and sacred self-care. Attention to bedroom magic and witchy feng shui, ensuring a beneficial flow of energy, will generate much of your happiness. In this chapter, you'll learn how to curate a relationship corner, a shrine to love that nurtures your partnership. There are also recipes for romantic dishes, and essential oils and blessed balms for conjuring bodily bliss. Your bedroom is also your sanctuary, however. One of the most important aspects of house magic is creating a haven of calm and tranquillity, where you can revitalize yourself and return to the outside world refreshed and ready to wield your special kind of magic.

Setting the mood

Of all the rooms in your home, the bedroom must be the real refuge, a place where you relax, refresh, and restore. It should be a center of self-care, a place where you pursue pleasures, such as reading a beloved novel undisturbed, and also a sacred center for your romantic relationship.

Ideally, your bedroom is where you unplug and recharge. You need to feel safest here, to feel able to "let your hair down," to be utterly yourself and utterly comfortable. There are days when you should stay in your pajamas and slippers, nurture your every desire, and do self-care spells. Let's admit it, we all face a lot of demands every day, so it's all the more important for your bedroom to be your personal retreat.

Make sure this room is beautiful to your eye as well as peaceful and deeply comfortable. Clutter will add a note of chaos to your bedroom, so keep the stacks of magazines and piles of sweaters under control to maintain the feeling of a safe haven. Every room should look and feel good to you, but your bedroom is the beating heart of your home. Keep it beautiful to your eye and pleasing to all your senses as well as those of your romantic partner. Make it the place where you can sleep, dream, meditate, read, convalesce, share your affection, and craft love magic.

Witchy feng shui for love

Surely one of the main reasons for clearing space in your home, and particularly your bedroom, is to make room for a happy love life. Before you attempt to enhance your prospects for love, you need to improve the flow of *chi*, or life energy, in the environment where you express your love. Try any or all of the following to help you to improve the *chi*:

- Remove all pictures of yourself in which you are alone.

- Remove all empty cups, jars, vases, and bottles.

- Remove all photographs of past lovers, or at least relegate them to another room.

- Make sure that decorative accessories are in even, rather than odd, numbers. This applies to candles, frames, pillows, and lamps.

- Display special feng shui love symbols, such as an open red fan, a pair of crystal lovebirds, and two red hearts.

- Use sumptuous, silky, and extremely comfortable fabrics and rich colors on your bed, in pink, orange, or red.

- Be extravagant when it comes to pillows: the more, the merrier (but remember to have even numbers, not odd ones, which disrupt your "love *chi*"), and tuck sweetly scented dried rose and lavender sachets into them.

Your relationship corner

In terms of pagan feng shui, as you walk into your bedroom, the relationship corner will be at the back right. Your love and romance energies should be nurtured there, and you might consider placing a shrine there to serve as your personal wellspring to turn to when you want to refresh these feelings of felicity.

Look at this area with a fresh eye. What is cluttering your love corner with stale energy? Half-empty perfume or cosmetics bottles could be impairing your relationship energy. You must clear unhappiness out of this space by getting rid of all unnecessary objects and tidying up any clutter.

To cleanse the area, ring a handbell anywhere clutter has accumulated, giving special attention to your bed and pillows. Here are a few tips:

- Never bring old pillows into a new home. These can cause poor sleep and bad dreams, carry old sexual energy, and kill a relationship.
- Never place your bed in the center of the room. This will cause anxiety and get in the way of a healthy relationship.
- Never place the bed so that its foot (the bottom of the bed) faces the door, as this brings very bad luck.
- To keep your romantic life fresh, make the bed every morning and change the linens often.

two by two

Place these objects in your bedroom to attract loving energy:

- Two rose quartz crystals of similar size
- Two red candles
- Images of two butterflies or a pair of lovebirds

Self-care sanctuary

As we know, the key to having a good relationship with anyone else, including a significant other, is to have a good relationship with yourself. Your bedroom is your temple, where you take sanctuary and from which you should emerge strong in spirit and body. I recommend that you perform this self-care spell at least once a month. Take a green candle, anoint it with bergamot or clary sage oil, and speak the following three times:

My health is my own: I am strong.

I choose joy and to live long.

No more illness, strife, or woe to me.

Harm to none: health to me. So mote it be.

Bed blessing

Put fresh cotton sheets on the bed and turn back the bedspread. In a red cup, mix ½ tsp each jasmine and rose essential oils. Hold it with both hands and speak:

In this bed, I show my love.

In this bed, I share my body.

In this bed, I give my heart.

In this bed, we are as one.

Here, my happiness lies as I give and live in total joy.

Blessed be to thee and me.

As you say "Blessed be," flick droplets of your bed blessing oil from your fingers all across the bed. The cotton sheets will absorb the droplets nicely and smell heavenly. (And the Eco Laundry Detergent recipe on page 42 will wash it all out when you are ready.) Now, lie down and roll around in the bed—after all, that's what it's there for!

The light of love

Ask any professional decorator the secret of a beautiful home and they will say that lighting is hugely important. For bedrooms it is even more important, since it sets the tone and mood. Your bedside lamp must be one that you love, and the bulb wattage should be enough to read by but not overly bright. Many metaphysical stores sell clay lamp rings that you can fill with essential oils, but you can also anoint your bulb before turning it on by gently dabbing it with a clean cloth dipped in an oil of your choice. Vanilla and amber are the ones I always turn to, but you should experiment until you find what you and your loved one prefer (see suggestions on page 74). You can also enhance the love energy of your lamp by draping the lampshade with a gorgeous scarf or cloth in a warm and amorous color, such as deep rose or smoldering orange. Of course, caution is advised, so don't leave it unattended and never let the fabric touch the bulb, only the shade.

After you have anointed and adorned your bedside lamp, pray aloud:

Aphrodite, aid me from
the heavens above!

Bring forth in me the wisdom of love.

Goddess bright, share with me your art.

Guide me in the ways of the heart.

I go in gratitude to you;
thank you for your light of love.

Now, adorn yourself and embody the goddess of love!

Aromatherapy Rituals for Romance and Rest

Essential oils have become wildly popular in the past few years. We witches are not surprised by this at all, since we have recognized their effectiveness for centuries. Essential oils are filled with the healing properties of herbs and the positive energy of Mother Nature, and they will give a true boost to your health, and that of your loved ones. Combine the power of these essences with massage and you will create real magic.

Custom massage oils can be made in minutes if you have the ingredients to hand. I am one lucky pagan to have a soap and candle store in my neighborhood: Juniper Tree in Berkeley, California. I am there twice a month picking up what I need, from candlewicks to essential and base oils and plain bath salts for my creations. Record your experiments with various oils in your Book of Shadows. After several moons, note which had the best results for you, and which you preferred.

Flower and herb-based aromatherapy essences can also be used in diffusers to infuse the air with the desired fragrance. Many of the most sensual essential oils combine well: Try a combination of amber and apple, ylang-ylang and sandalwood, clary sage and rose, or almond and neroli. If you're using a candle diffuser, rose or orange-blossom water is an aromatic and romantic alternative to plain water in the diffuser cup.

eight oils of enchantment

These essential oils are excellent choices for anointing lamps as well as yourself:

- *Cinnamon* is energetic, spicy, and warm. It stimulates the mind as well as the body.

- *Ginger* is vigorous and revitalizing, and heightens desire and comfort.

- *Jasmine* sparks sensuality and inspires feelings of positivity, confidence, and pure bliss.

- *Lavender* is soothing, calming, nurturing, and relaxing.

- *Orange* is a light, citrusy oil that restores balance and lifts moods, enhancing playful emotions.

- *Rose* brings youthfulness, enhances self-esteem, aids circulation, and relieves tension.

- *Sandalwood* is a woody aroma that relieves tension and relaxes tense muscles.

- *Ylang-ylang's* sweet, floral aroma is used as an aphrodisiac; it is relaxing and reduces worry and anxiety.

Conjuring with carrier oils

A carrier oil is a vegetable oil that is used to dilute essential oils without diminishing the effect of the essence. It ensures that essential oils used topically are comfortable on the skin. Each essential oil carries specific vibrations that hold much curative power. These base oils support other ingredients, including essential oils, but can also be a vessel for healing in themselves.

Apricot kernel oil, with its warmth and resilience, is especially good for women. Apricot protects love and nurtures women at every age and stage of life.

Avocado oil is thick, dense, and earthy, a powerful element in any love potion. It is also excellent for drawing forth money and is helpful in business and financial matters.

Borage oil brings a connection with the higher mind, as well as courage, a sense of honor, and the ability to cope with whatever life sends your way. It is said to encourage truth and resolution in legal and relationship problems. If you feel you are being deceived, turn to borage.

Evening primrose oil abets clairvoyance and paranormal gifts. It will help you to see clearly.

Grape-seed oil is regarded by some as the "food of the gods" because of the way it augments spiritual growth. This should be one of the oils that you turn to for anointing yourself or any statuary of gods and goddesses before rituals.

Jojoba oil absorbs extremely well into the skin, bearing anything it is mixed with. It is also a remarkable anointing oil. It should be used in recipes that help to deal with depression and support perseverance in hardship.

Olive oil was named "liquid gold" by the ancient Greek poet Homer, and rightly so: It is about vitality, money, success, and joyfulness.

Sunflower oil is permeated with the energy of our sun, and is powerful and life-giving. Use it when you desire rapid growth and amplification of positive energy.

Sweet almond oil is a gentle, all-purpose oil ready to increase the energy of other ingredients.

Tranquillity meditation

Sandalwood, lavender, and clary sage make a deeply relaxing blend with a warm, soothing scent.

Mix the oils in a tightly capped blue or brown bottle. Shake well and pour a little of the mix into the palm of your hand to warm it before using. Rub it lightly onto your shoulder and neck as well as your temples and wrists. Sit comfortably, close your eyes, and breathe deeply. Chant aloud:

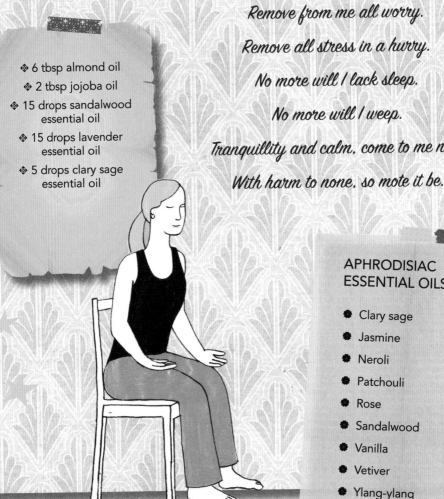

- ❖ 6 tbsp almond oil
- ❖ 2 tbsp jojoba oil
- ❖ 15 drops sandalwood essential oil
- ❖ 15 drops lavender essential oil
- ❖ 5 drops clary sage essential oil

Remove from me all worry.

Remove all stress in a hurry.

No more will I lack sleep.

No more will I weep.

Tranquillity and calm, come to me now.

With harm to none, so mote it be.

APHRODISIAC ESSENTIAL OILS

- Clary sage
- Jasmine
- Neroli
- Patchouli
- Rose
- Sandalwood
- Vanilla
- Vetiver
- Ylang-ylang

Beltane bliss balm

Beltane (May 1) is the most romantic day of the pagan calendar, and with this blissful combination of oils you can summon the spirit of Beltane then or on any day of the year. Amber, rose, and sandalwood create a sensual scent that lingers on your skin for hours.

Mix the oils in a brown or dark blue tightly capped bottle and shake well. You now have an aphrodisiac in a bottle, so use it as a bath oil or a perfume, or for magic cottage aromatherapy in your home.

Additional romantic touches include fresh flowers, which can be used in creative ways. In Indonesia, lilies and orange blossom are scattered on the bed of newlyweds. You can also make a trail of blossoms for your lover to follow, sprinkle rose petals on your bed, or surround your bed with a garland of flowers. Plenty of pillows for lounging, sensuous silk or chenille throws for staying cozy, and your favorite mood-setting music all help to cast a spell of romance.

- ❧ 6 tbsp almond oil
- ❧ 2 tbsp sandalwood oil
- ❧ 3 drops rose essential oil
- ❧ 5 drops amber essential oil

Earth goddess sandalwood salts

Sandalwood, jasmine, and vetiver are all rich, earthy floral scents that go well together. The right combination of these essential oils evokes a romantic mood. In addition to aiding focus, calm, and sensuality, sandalwood can help your wishes come true.

Pour the Epsom salts into a large bowl with the baking soda (bicarbonate of soda), and mix well. Add the essential oils and stir until the scents are infused thoroughly. While you are running a hot bath, put the salts in under the faucet (tap) to maximize the release of the oils' perfume. Relax and enjoy—and be sure to make a wish. If possible, air-dry yourself instead of using a towel. As the witches of olden days said, "Go sky-clad!"

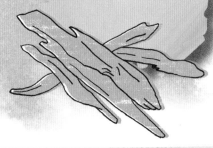

- ½ cup (90 g) Epsom salts
- 1 cup (140 g) baking soda (bicarbonate of soda)
- 6 drops sandalwood essential oil
- 2 drops jasmine essential oil

time is on your side spell

A gift of a clock is lucky. Luckier still is to hear two clocks chiming together at a happy moment. If you are kissing, happy in company, meeting someone you like, concluding a business deal, or launching a project, or indeed in the midst of any other hopeful occasion, and you hear two clocks striking together, link fingers with the other person, or kiss them on the cheek (if it seems appropriate!). Say:

Two clocks have struck.

'Tis set for luck.

Take careful note of the hour. For the next two days, observe the hour again and think of the event that has just taken place; wish hard for luck on that matter once again. Good luck will come to you, exactly at the right time.

Coconut milk bath

- 2 drops ylang-ylang essential oil
- 3 drops orange essential oil
- 1 can (13½ fl oz/400 ml) coconut milk

Coconut milk makes for a rich, moisturizing soak that leaves your skin as smooth as silk. The exhilarating fragrance of the orange and ylang-ylang will render you irresistible.

Mix the essential oils and the coconut milk in a large bowl or pitcher (jug) and add to the warm running water as you fill the bathtub. Soak to your heart's content.

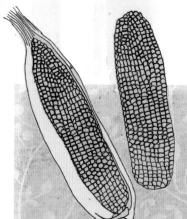

CHAPTER 5

Edible Landscaping

Growing an Enchanted Garden and Many Magical Recipes

Growing plants will definitely bring pleasure, and a sense of calm. When I feel stressed, I head outside and do some weeding. It is my therapy and I can immediately see the profit of my labors. The bigger my compost pile grows with weeds, the happier I am. I intend the same for you. With your enchanted garden, whether inside or out back, you are quite literally growing a bounty of blessings. It is truly satisfying to be able to create delicious dishes from herbs and vegetables grown by your own hand, too. A garden-to-table meal served to your loved ones, no matter how humble the fare, is more delectable than fancy food, because it contains the very special ingredient of magic.

Have your garden and eat it, too!

Gardening—even if it is only a hanging basket of cherry tomatoes, a heavenly-smelling lemon tree on your deck, or a windowsill filled with herb pots—offers us a very human way to live, grounded in nature and connected to Mother Earth, who provides all. I love seeing community gardens in large cities, each urban gardener busy with their own productive and beautiful plot. For years, I gardened quite happily with an array of pots and a deck full of herbs, vegetables, pansies, and lobelia.

Many gardens have lawns, which need a lot of maintenance: Unless they are constantly mowed and manicured, patchy, weed-filled grass can greatly reduce your curb appeal. Besides wasting water and requiring a lot of effort, grass in your yard doesn't offer you anything back for all the demands it makes on your time and money. It also tempts many gardeners to use chemicals, which are bad for us all, especially the birds and the bees. Get creative and go at least a little wild. My next-door neighbors overturned and tilled their front lawn and planted potatoes, beets, asparagus, and squash. They love going into the front yard and harvesting fresh vegetables for their daily meals. The squash actually have beautiful foliage, and the flowers are stunning and even edible. Last year, one grew to "Giant Pumpkin" size, and it became the talk of the neighborhood as we watched it grow and grow. Needless to say, they had the best jack-o'-lantern on the block, and made some fantastic pies to boot. I am heartened to see the new gardening philosophy of growing vegetables, roots, herbs, and berries right beside roses and lilies. It is gorgeous and supports the bee populations, to which we owe so much.

What vegetables do you love? What are your favorite salad greens? The first rule is to plant what you will actually eat and feel proud to serve to guests. In your Book of Shadows, make a list of your preferred herbs, greens, vegetables (including root vegetables), fruit, and herbs. Now, strike out anything you can buy really cheaply, since there is no sense in using valuable space for something that is easily available for less than it will cost you to grow it.

It's also important to check out your soil type. The five basic types are sandy, clay, peat, silt, and the ideal, loam. To find out what kind you have, pick up a chunk of your soil the size of a marble and roll it into a ball. If your soil is silty, you'll begin to feel the silky-smooth texture, which won't roll into any shape. Clay soil easily forms a little ball that will keep its shape. If the soil does not form a ball and keeps falling apart, it is sandy. Loam will form a ball only if you keep putting pressure on it, and peat is simply too loose to form anything. Soil type will inform your choice of what to grow. For example, carrots need deep, rich soil to grow well, so if your lot has shallow, sandy soil, cross them off your list and try surface crops such as potatoes and beets instead. If you're unsure about your soil type or what will suit it best, consult a general gardening guide or look online, where you will find lots of helpful advice.

Easy-peasy peas and veggies

The guide I recommend is Niki Jabbour's *The Year-Round Vegetable Gardener: How to Grow Your Own Food 365 Days a Year, No Matter Where You Live.* Jabbour learned how to grow "anything anywhere" from living in Nova Scotia, a tough environment for gardeners. I live in California, but still I turn to her book all the time. As the book's title might suggest, her advice is excellent for any kind of zone, soil, and climate.

Here are the vegetables that anyone can grow, even beginners:

Lettuce leaves for your salads are the easiest edible crop to grow, and so quick—some varieties are ready to harvest in weeks! Choose a seed mix that will give you a variety of leaves for different tastes, colors, and textures. For best results, sow in stages—a couple of rows every few weeks throughout the summer—so you get a continuous supply, rather than too many all at once. Once you are a pro with lettuce, try growing spinach and arugula (rocket) to add to your salad bowl.

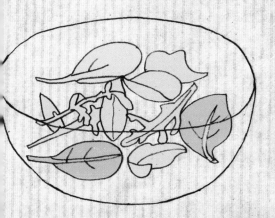

Peas are a trouble-free crop that can handle cooler weather, so you can skip the step of starting the seedlings indoors. Simply sow the seeds in the ground from spring onward, and watch them thrive. The plants will need support, so put in stakes or chicken wire attached to posts and occasionally wind the stems around as they grow. Harvest your fresh peas in the summer—the more you pick, the more will grow.

Onions are problem-free and easy to propagate from seed. After your seedlings sprout, thin them to 1 in. (2.5 cm) apart, then thin them again 4 weeks later to 6 in. (15 cm) apart. Onions are a staple for cooking, so you and your family will be grateful once you have established an onion patch in your kitchen garden.

Potatoes and beets offer a high return for your labor. To me, the best way to grow both is the world's laziest way to garden; I remember reading about it when I was ten in a book by Thalassa Cruso, a pioneering organic gardener. I was fascinated that you could grow root vegetables without even needing to turn any soil. You can grow potatoes, yams, beets, and so on under straw! Simply cut up mature potatoes that have "eyes" (the fleshy growths sprouting from the skin of the potato), making sure each piece has at least one eye. This will give a new potato plant after you "plant" or place the seed-potato chunks on the ground. Now, put loose straw over the pieces and between all the rows to a depth of at least 6 in. (15 cm). When the seed pieces start growing, your potato sprouts will emerge through the straw, which will begin to break down and turn into a soil-enriching layer of compost. Don't add any more straw, as that will make life difficult for the growing plants. You don't need to do anything after planting. How easy is that? Cruso also said that you could do the same under wet, shredded newspaper, but straw is more organic.

Radishes are enjoying new popularity thanks to Korean and Japanese cuisine. They add a fun pop of spicy, tangy flavor to soups, stews, tempura, and salads, as well as tasting great on their own. They can grow equally well in the ground or in a pot, and they like a lot of sun and well-drained soil. They are also a vegetable that will produce several crops per season. If you keep the soil moist, you'll soon have big, beautiful radishes to brighten any dish.

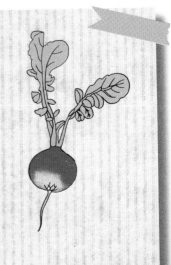

Green beans are the opposite of the low-maintenance beets and potatoes, as they need poles for support. However, an easier path to a nice crop of green beans is to grow them in a 5-gallon (20-liter) container. Once the bean vines are 4–5 ft (1.2–1.5 m) tall, place a pole or stake carefully in the pot and allow the vines to wind around it. Soon you'll have a pot of beans that even Grandma might recognize as a favorite side dish for any occasion.

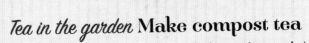

Tea in the garden Make compost tea

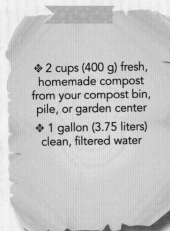

❖ 2 cups (400 g) fresh, homemade compost from your compost bin, pile, or garden center

❖ 1 gallon (3.75 liters) clean, filtered water

Compost tea is a marvelous way to feed your plants and give them extra nutrients in a wholly natural way that is free of chemicals. You want to feed your friends and family clean, pesticide-free produce, so start out organic and you will soon have a garden that produces healthy food.

Put the compost and water in a large bucket and place out of direct heat or cold—I use my shed, but a garage will also do nicely. Let your compost tea "brew" for a week and give it a stir every other day. When the time is up, strain out the dirt and pour the liquid into your watering can—the perfect garden teapot—to serve up some serious nutrients to your plants.

green witchery: rules of (green) thumb

- Always grow vegetables and fruit that you and your family love to eat.

- Your kitchen garden should be a sunny, open spot that is easy for you to see and tend.

- Check your soil type, and use containers or raised beds if it is too poor, too dry, or too damp and swampy. Of course, a compost pile can fix most soil problems soon enough.

- Preparation is everything: Remove rocks and weeds, and loosen the soil so it can "breathe."

- Develop your garden soil by mixing in compost. Once the plants are established, serve them compost tea (see opposite).

- Patience is a virtue. Don't sow too early: Wait until the soil is warmed up in spring.

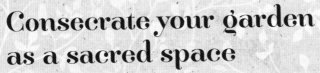

Consecrate your garden as a sacred space

You can sanctify your garden by "casting" a magic circle there, drawing it in the air with concentrated energy in order to make your yard a sacred space where you can perform your rituals, cast spells, and conduct blessings and rites. Here, you can also call upon the gods and goddesses, and invoke ancestors and benevolent spirits.

Wiccan tradition specifies that the circle for a ritual or spell must have a diameter of 9 ft (2.75 m). However, you can expand the circle to accommodate a big patch of vegetables and plants, a large group of people, or just yourself. Casting a circle in the area where you garden will imbue your crops with magic. For indoor gardening, you can do the same to sanctify your space and the plants in it. Many Wiccans and other pagans cast a circle for spell work and to enclose every seasonal sabbat celebration.

This sacred circle of my garden is where I feel most at peace. If I am troubled, I can go outside to meditate, or sometimes just "be." When I first moved to my witchy cottage, the backyard was dry and dead, with a couple of trees clinging to life in the prolonged drought. As a dedicated eco pagan, I devised a bucket system for watering the garden with cooled bathwater. After years of hauling buckets every day, I now have a lovely, lush garden that produces an abundance of vegetables and fruit. It is truly filled with blessings, and I can feel the presence of our greatest goddess, Mother Earth, in every corner. Honeybees and butterflies are regular visitors, and a family of bluebirds took up residence in one of the trees. This is what I wish for you: your personal Paradise, your very own Eden in your own backyard.

Bluebird of happiness wish

Bluebirds have become known in many cultures as a symbol of happiness. The robin is also associated with signs of cheerfulness and joy. If you see a bluebird or a robin, you should immediately make a wish: It must be something unselfish, and not dependent on anyone else.

As the bird flies off, think of what your heart truly desires, breathe deeply, and set your wish ascending. If you see the bird again within a few days, in exactly the same place, your wish will certainly be granted.

other magical wings and prayers

- *Crow feathers* indicate loss and mourning. Try not to be frightened, but look at them as indicators of the cycles of life, death, and rebirth.

- *Hummingbird feathers* bring joy, beauty, and bliss. Take time out to enjoy yourself and be with the people you love.

- *Swan feathers* are the sign of grace. Since swans mate for life, a swan feather can also indicate that a soul mate or good relationship is on the horizon.

- *Yellowhammer feathers* symbolize hearth and home. Seeing a yellowhammer feather on your path means you will have a happy new home.

- *Magpie feathers* are just plain good medicine for any kind of illness: attach one to your wand, or place it on your healing altar. These birds have many meanings in our culture—you may have been taught to be wary of them, and some people still salute them—but, in fact, they bring purification.

Effortless herbs

All these herbs will grow happily in containers on a patio or balcony, and even on the kitchen windowsill. Start an herb garden this year and you'll never look back.

Basil is beloved because it's so delectable and so versatile. It is easily grown in pots. Take care to remove the growing tip when the plants are about 6 in. (15 cm) high, for bushier growth. Plant it out in the garden when the weather gets warmer and repot for the fall (autumn) so that you have a constant crop of this sacred, savory herb. Basil prefers full sun and a sheltered spot.

Chives come from the onion family and have slim, pointed leaves. Sow seeds directly in the ground in early spring. Chives grow best in a sunny spot with rich soil, so keep the plants watered. They also produce pretty purple or pink, perfectly round flowers, so these herbs are gorgeous in the garden and very palatable on the plate.

Coriander is a very versatile herb for the kitchen and grows well in the garden or in pots. Seeds can take weeks to germinate, and the plants are fairly short-lived, so sow seeds every few weeks to get you through the season. It is a bit fussy and can "bolt" when stressed, which means it produces flowers and seeds and not enough of the flavorful leaves. Make sure it is watered well, and reap regularly before it goes to seed.

Mint is a marvel. It spreads beautifully once it has really taken root. If space is a concern, plant your mint in pots to contain the roots and stop it taking over. Mint is a bit fussy about soil, so you'll need to repot it every year or so to keep it happy. Stand the pots in full sun or partial shade and pinch out any flower buds to encourage more leafy growth.

Oregano loves a Mediterranean climate and conditions, so plant yours in a warm, sunny spot with light soil. It has pretty pink flowers and makes great ground cover at the front of borders. Don't allow this herb to get too tall or go to seed, though: Pinch out its top shoots to keep it bushy and lush, and you'll get more of this tasty treat to harvest.

Parsley This herb can be slow to germinate, so try soaking the seeds in water overnight before planting, to speed it up. The best place to grow parsley is in rich, moist soil in full sun or partial shade.

Rosemary has many culinary and magical uses. Lucky for us, it grows vigorously. It can be trimmed in early summer to keep it in shape and stop it from getting too woody. The scent is wonderful in dishes and in spells.

Sage is a marvelous herb for cooking, and is truly easy to grow. It doesn't like wet ground, so plant it in a sunny spot in rich, well-drained soil. There are several varieties to choose from, including some with colored leaves. Harvest the leaves regularly to encourage more to grow. This versatile herb is not only a culinary pleasure but also very important in magic.

Thyme is a cousin of mint and grows much lower to the ground; it is one of the most fragrant herbs and will add great flavor to your cooking. Plant it to remove melancholy from your home and garden. If your front yard gets afternoon sun, plant wooly thyme and you'll come home after work to a perfume paradise that will instantly cheer and comfort you.

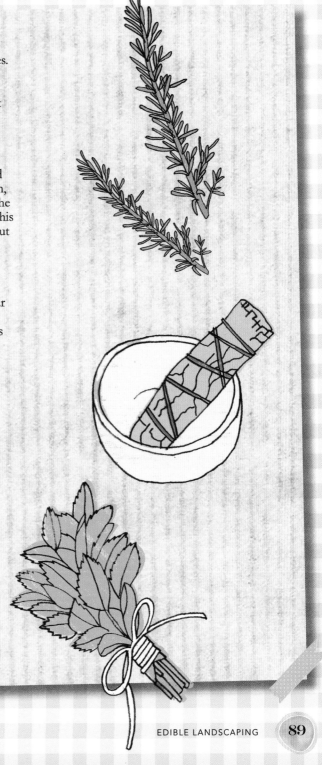

Lunar almanac
Moon signs of the times

The astrological signs of the moon are of great significance. Each moon sign has special meaning that has been passed down through the centuries. Ancient and medieval people paid strict attention to moon phases and moon signs for planting, harvesting, and canning and preserving produce for the long winter. Here is a guide to each sign, with tried-and-true lore from olden days along with applications for today's rituals.

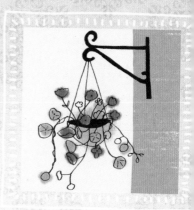

Aries is a barren and dry sign that is perfect for planting, weeding, haying, and harvesting. Moon in Aries is the optimum time for starting a big project, such as digging a garden plot for the first time or starting an herb garden in your kitchen.

Taurus is an earthy, moist sign that is excellent for planting root crops such as potatoes, beets, and peanuts. Moon in Taurus is a good time for buying a garden plot or farm, or investing in your home. It is also the best time for planting leafy vegetables, such as lettuce, spinach, and cabbage.

Gemini is another dry sign that is the best time for mowing, cutting, and getting rid of weeds or pests. Melon seeds thrive if they are planted now. Since communication is at a peak during Gemini Moon, it is also a great time for a garden party!

Cancer is a fruitful watery sign that is conducive to planting; in fact, it is the most productive sign of all. Hearth and home are the focus now, and Moon in Cancer is a good time for lunar rituals.

Leo is the driest and least fertile of all moon signs, good only for cutting and mowing. Leo Moon is good for weeding and removing "volunteers," such as thorny brambles, that sprout uninvited.

Virgo is both damp and barren, but a great time for cultivation. Virgo Moon is good for hard work and major projects. This moon sign is the perfect time for all kinds of healing spell work and for making tinctures, tonics, floral waters, and essences.

Libra is both wet and fruitful, and is wonderful for grains, vines, root crops, and flowers. This is the time to beautify your home and garden and add refinement to your sacred space. Moon in Libra is the most favorable time for working with fragrant flowers, vines, and shrubs.

Scorpio, humid and bountiful, is good for all types of planting. This is an especially good time to work with fruit trees, including grafting. Tomatoes are best transplanted during Scorpio Moon.

Sagittarius is another fire sign that is a poor time for planting and is best spent harvesting and storing. It is an excellent time for working and improving the soil, and good for reaping root crops.

Capricorn is an earth sign that is also wet, and is excellent for grafting, pruning, and planting trees and shrubs. It is also an ideal time for planting root crops. Rituals relating to future plans and visioning can be started now, and trees can be saved and healed.

 Aquarius is an infertile and parched moon time that is best for harvesting, weeding, and dispelling pests. The Aquarian Moon is very good for storing, canning, and preserving. Onions thrive when planted during this sign.

 Pisces is fecund and fruitful and is good for all kinds of planting. It is remarkable for fruit of all kinds. The highly sensitive Moon in Pisces is great for spells and charms.

Dirt spell Black forest earth magic

I learned this multipurpose blessing from Ruth, a Holocaust survivor, poet, priestess, and all-around goddess, who lives in what is truly an enchanted cottage in the forest. She brought this wisdom from Europe, where it was passed down to her through a long line of wise women. It is the simplest of spells, and that might be the secret to its extraordinary effectiveness. It can be used to help an ailing loved one; if you need money; to solve legal problems, job troubles, or romantic woes; or to summon any help you need that is for the good of all. It is excellent for earth magic and gardening magic, so try it before you plant any crops.

Go into your yard or garden, put both your hands into the earth, and scoop up a handful of dirt. Hold the soil in both hands in front of you and repeat three times aloud:

> *Mother, I need your help.*
>
> *Please send _____.*
>
> *Thank you. Blessings all.*

Then stand in front of a flower bed, or anywhere that the soil will be useful and helpful, and throw it over your left shoulder.

Recipes from your magic garden
The kitchen witch's table

One of the most rewarding aspects of gardening is serving meals made from herbs, vegetables, and fruit grown by your own hand to your friends and family. All the care, thought, planning, and love that you put into your plants will come through on the plate in fabulous flavors and healthy organic food, and, most important, all your meals will be permeated with magic.

❖ 1 cup (75 g) fresh basil
❖ ¾ cup (170 ml) virgin olive oil (or safflower or canola/rapeseed oil)

Makes ¾ cup

OTHER INFUSED OILS
These herbs also make fantastic infused oils using the same method:

● Chives

● Cilantro (coriander)

● Parsley

● Rosemary

● Tarragon

Infusion of prosperity
Basil oil

Infusion is a trendy, yet incredibly easy, cooking method that brings the flavors of one food—in this case, fresh herbs—to another, such as oil. The next chapter of this book goes into magical infusions in more depth. Ideally, gather fresh herbs from your own kitchen garden, but any farmers' market or organic grocery will stock green herbs. For the best and purest flavor, use fresh herbs. They are best shortly after they are picked, and must be used before they wilt and lose their flavor, nutrients, and healing energy.

Rinse the basil thoroughly in cold water, pat dry gently with paper towels, and chop coarsely. Prepare a large bowl of iced water, then place the basil in a metal colander and dip into boiling water for 10 seconds. Plunge the colander into the iced water and drain well, then gently pat dry. Pour the oil into a sealable jar or bottle and add the basil. Seal and set aside in a cool, dark place. After 3–5 days, the fresh, bright green flavor of the basil will have infused into the oil. Refrigerate your basil-infused oil and it will keep for up to 4 months. Use it liberally on roasts, salads, cooked vegetables and soups. Basil not only gives a delicious taste, but also brings prosperity.

Lovely love apples Fried green tomatoes

- 1 large egg
- ½ cup (110 ml) buttermilk
- ½ cup (70 g) all-purpose (plain) flour
- ½ cup (90 g) cornmeal
- 1 tsp salt
- ½ tsp freshly ground black pepper
- 3 medium-size green heirloom tomatoes, sliced
- 1 cup olive or vegetable oil

Serves 6

Tomatoes are a guardian plant, so growing them in your yard creates a protective field around your home and grounds. All that and they are good for you, too. This specialty of Southern cuisine has gone global, and little wonder, for it is simply scrumptious. Using heirloom green tomatoes adds greatly to the taste. What puts it over the top, though, is that tomatoes—historically referred to as "love apples"—bring love. These fried tomatoes are mouthwatering on their own, but if you make BLTs, this recipe will quickly become a household favorite. It is a gorgeous classic that will bring more love into your life. Serve it on a first date, and there will definitely be a second!

Beat the egg in a medium bowl, and stir in the buttermilk. Put half the flour in a shallow bowl and set both bowls aside. In a large, shallow bowl, combine the rest of the flour, the cornmeal, salt, and pepper. Take each "love apple" slice and dredge it in the flour, then dip it in the egg mix. Finally, dip it in the cornmeal and flour mix, making sure to coat the tomato well.

Pour the oil into a cast-iron skillet (frying pan) to a depth of ½ in. (1 cm) and heat to 375°F/190°C, checking the temperature using an oil thermometer. Drop the tomatoes in (in batches if needed, depending on the size of your pan) and cook for 2 minutes on each side, or until golden. Drain on paper towels and sprinkle with salt to taste. If you have any leftovers— very unlikely!—fried tomatoes are delicious in sandwiches or on buttered cheese toast.

Summer in a bowl
Herbed potato beet salad

- ❖ 2 small golden beets (beetroot)
- ❖ 2 lb (900 g) red potatoes
- ❖ ¾ cup (35 g) chopped red onion
- ❖ ½ cup (110 ml) fat-free plain yogurt or sour cream
- ❖ ½ cup (110 ml) mayonnaise
- ❖ 2 tbsp each fresh dill and fresh chives, chopped
- ❖ 2 tbsp lemon juice
- ❖ 1 tsp salt
- ❖ 2 tsp apple cider vinegar
- ❖ chive oil, to serve

Serves 6

This simple salad is a great centerpiece for any picnic or pagan potluck. Use one of your prettiest bowls to serve it.

Place the beets and potatoes in a large pot and add cold water to cover. Put the lid on the pot and bring to a boil, then simmer for about 35 minutes, until tender. Drain and cool. Set the beets aside. Peel the potatoes and cut into 1 in. (2.5 cm) cubes. (I like to leave the skin on at least half of the potatoes, for color and also to get those additional nutrients.)

Combine the cooled, chopped potatoes with the onion in a large serving bowl and toss gently. In a separate bowl, combine the remaining ingredients to make the dressing. Spoon the mixture over the potatoes and onions and mix gently until the potatoes are coated with the dressing.

Peel the beets and slice into thin golden coins. Place them on top of the potatoes in a circular pattern. Cover the bowl and refrigerate for 6 hours. Finally, drizzle a little infused chive oil on top for a finishing touch of pure herbal flavor.

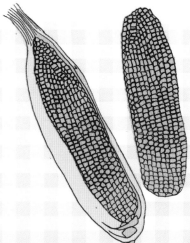

Amazing maize
Baked corn pudding

This treat truly represents autumnal abundance and is a wonderful dish to bring to a Harvest Moon Feast. Not many of us have enough real estate to grow our own corn (otherwise known as maize), but this recipe is so tasty that you may want to give up the front lawn and get a crop going so that you have the freshest possible corn. In winter, you can use frozen corn (thaw before using). If you don't have fresh chives to hand, use the green part of a few scallions (spring onions) instead.

Preheat the oven to 350°F/180°C/Gas 4 and combine the corn, chives, thyme, salt, and pepper in a medium bowl. In another medium bowl, mix the milk, cream cheese, and egg. Add the milk mixture to the corn mixture, and stir well to combine. Pour into an 11 x 7 in. (28 x 18 cm) baking dish coated with oil. Bake for 55 minutes, or until the top of the pudding is golden brown.

- 3 cups (375 g) corn kernels (about 6 ears)
- ¼ cup (25 g) chopped fresh chives
- 1 tbsp chopped fresh thyme
- ¾ tsp salt
- ¼ tsp freshly ground black pepper
- 1½ cups (335 ml) low-fat (semi-skimmed) milk
- 2 tbsp cream cheese
- 1 large egg, lightly beaten
- oil, for greasing

Serves 6

Healing spell in a bowl
Ginger carrot soup

- 1 lb (450 g) carrots, cleaned and sliced; set aside the carrot greens
- 4 cups (900 ml) water
- 1 tbsp fresh ginger, chopped
- 1 large garlic clove, peeled and crushed
- ¼ tsp crushed red pepper, plus extra to garnish
- ½ tsp salt
- 1 lemon

Serves 6

Ginger is an energetic herb and adds fire and spice to anything it is used for, whether a healing cup of tea, a salad, a savory dish, or this special soup. Ginger root is a quickener and is renowned for making magic happen faster. It is also medicinal and helps to soothe the symptoms of colds, congestion, flu, and fever. Combine it with carrots, which are wonderfully grounding and bring what is hidden to light, and you have a simple, soothing soup that can ground and center you, heal you, and make you more psychic—and all at a faster pace. And, as if that isn't enough, it is pleasing to the senses in every way.

Set one carrot aside, put the rest in a big pot, and add the water. Bring to a boil, then simmer on a medium heat for 20–25 minutes, adding the ginger, garlic, red pepper, and salt after 5 minutes. Meanwhile, place the last carrot on your altar (see opposite for how to imbue this recipe with extra magic). When the carrots are tender, transfer them with their water to a blender and blend until smooth. Stir in several squeezes of lemon juice and pour into bowls or mugs. Garnish with a few chopped carrot greens and a sprinkling of crushed red pepper.

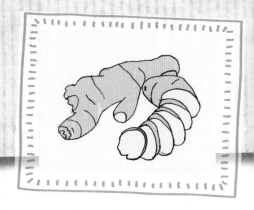

Instilling magic into healing food

Healing spells are the highest "earth magic." The rituals that create both soundness of body and clarity of mind are eminently practical. They are a wonderful mix of gardening, herb lore, minding the moon and sky, and heeding ancient folk wisdom. In crafting healing you are using your magic in conjunction with the properties of the herbs—a powerful combination. It is a subtle process, and one that grows more effective over time through repeated practice. In the case of Ginger Carrot Soup, you are transforming lovingly made soup into a medicinal meal. To do so, light a green candle on your kitchen altar or table. Place the carrot that was on your altar beside the candle while you prepare the meal; afterward, you can use it for another meal. While the soup is simmering, stir it widdershins (counterclockwise) and chant aloud:

Nature, Mother of us all,

I ask you to remove this sickness and pall.

May the healing power of this food

Brighten our health and our home to the good.

Blessed be.

Beer bread blessings Cheesy beer loaf

You'll be invited to every pagan party after you bring a loaf of this cheesy crowd-pleaser. This blessing-filled bread goes wonderfully with soups and stews, as well as dips and, as you might guess, a cold beer.

❖ 3 cups (420 g) self-rising (self-raising) flour

❖ ½ cup (100 g) sugar

❖ 12 oz. (350 ml) bottle of beer

❖ ¾ cup (90 g) grated sharp Cheddar cheese

❖ 2 tbsp chopped fresh chives

❖ ¼ cup (60 ml) melted butter

❖ oil, for greasing

Makes 1 loaf

Preheat the oven to 350°F/180°C/Gas 4 and lightly oil a 2 lb (900 g) loaf pan (tin). Put the flour, sugar, beer, cheese, and chives into a large bowl and stir well. Pour the mixture into the pan and bake for 45 minutes. Carefully pull out the oven rack so that you can pour the butter over the top of the bread, then bake it for 10 minutes more. Remove from the oven, turn out of the pan onto a wire rack, and serve warm or cold.

Enchanted garden Vegetable pasta pot

Carrots are more than just a healthy snack for lunchtime or a colorful crunch in your salad: They are grounding and bring clarity of thought and mind, and they are also good for romance. Nothing adds freshness to a dish like fresh mint. For this stress-free garden bowl, the combination of mint with fresh peas and baby carrots provides irresistible pops of flavor, not to mention lots of nutritional value. Why drown your pasta in oodles of sauce when veggies from your garden simply tossed in oil are absolutely delicious?

❖ 1 bunch baby carrots, peeled and sliced lengthways

❖ 1 lb (450 g) box of pasta noodles or shells

❖ 1½ cups (225 g) freshly picked shelled peas (in winter, frozen peas work nicely)

❖ 2 tbsp olive oil

❖ ¼ tsp each salt and freshly ground black pepper

❖ ⅓ cup (25 g) fresh mint leaves, rinsed

Serves 6

Preheat the oven to 425°F/220°C/Gas 7. Place the carrots on a baking sheet with 1 tbsp of the oil, and the salt and black pepper, and roast in the oven for 15–18 minutes. Meanwhile, cook the pasta in boiling salted water for 10 minutes, or according to the directions on the box. Add the peas for the last 2 minutes of cooking. Drain, reserving ¼ cup (60 ml) of the pasta water. Return the pasta and peas to the pot. Add the roasted carrots to the pot with the reserved pasta water. Toss in the mint leaves and stir in the rest of the oil.

Ingredients

- ❖ ½ small cabbage, grated
- ❖ 2 carrots, grated
- ❖ 1 cup (150 g) snap (sugar snap) peas, sliced
- ❖ 1 cup (150 g) radishes, thinly sliced
- ❖ 6 scallions (spring onions), thinly sliced
- ❖ 2 tbsp chopped hazelnuts
- ❖ 2 tbsp chopped fresh parsley
- ❖ 1 tbsp poppy seeds
- ❖ juice of ½ lemon
- ❖ 3 tbsp extra virgin olive oil
- ❖ ¼ tsp each salt and freshly ground black pepper

Serves 4

Kitchen witch winter salad

Crunchy coleslaw

In a large serving bowl, combine the cabbage, carrots, peas, radishes, scallions (spring onions), hazelnuts, parsley, and poppy seeds. Set aside while you make the dressing.

In a small bowl, whisk the lemon juice, oil, salt, and pepper together well. Pour over the vegetables and toss until the dressing is well distributed.

magical correspondences of nuts

- *Acorns:* Transformation and spirituality with the energy of the moon
- *Almonds:* Healing, money, and the energy of Mercury
- *Cashews:* Abundance and the energy of the sun
- *Chestnuts:* Love and higher consciousness with the sun's energy
- *Coconuts:* Protection, psychic awareness, and spirituality with the moon's energy
- *Hazelnuts:* Connection to the fairy world, clarity, wisdom, psychism, healing, and fertility
- *Macadamias:* Plentitude and wealth, and the energy of Jupiter
- *Peanuts:* Better luck and more money with the energy of Jupiter
- *Pecans:* A new job and the energy of Mercury
- *Pine nuts:* Physical strength and courage with the energy of Mars
- *Walnuts:* Mental acuity, connection to deities, and the energy of the sun

CHAPTER 6

The Pagan Pantry

DIY Pickles, Jams, Preserves, and Liqueurs to Enjoy All Year Round

The great C.S. Lewis's wardrobe portal to the magical land of Narnia has nothing on a witch's pantry: They, too, are gateways to a land of enchantment. Here, you'll find stores of food and medicine, ingredients for spell work and all manner of homemade preserves, pickles, infusions, wines, liqueurs, and other yummy stuff made with a special added dash of magic. Any good witch knows that the best ingredients can be found in your kitchen or your own backyard. Many plants that are now thought of as weeds have great healing powers and magical properties, and have even become quite trendy at fancy restaurants—to the great amusement of my farming relatives.

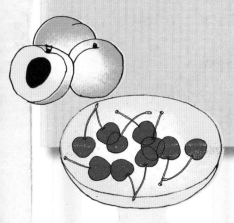

Kitchen-cabinet elixirs and infusions

The wise women in my family encouraged me to dedicate a corner of the pantry to kitchen-cabinet cures. My great aunts had come of age in the Great Depression, when there was no money for new clothes or shoes, let alone store-bought medicine or trips to the doctor. Fortunately, healing wisdom was passed down from one generation to the next. My great aunts also had green thumbs and were inveterate gardeners who grew vegetables by the bushel, as well as riotous beds filled with colorful flowers. Enthusiastic proponents of the virtue of thrift, they believed that flowers were not just for decoration, and they used them for jellies, hand-sewn sachets, vinegars, flower water, and medicinal purposes. When a neighbor lost a loved one, a bottle of honeysuckle essence was tucked into a lovingly packed gift basket with a sympathetic note. Hard times and worrisome burdens were met with lemon balm and thyme accompanied by a cup of herbal tea. These women lived through the last world war and economic disaster, but they handled everything with a can-do attitude and a pantry full of love.

Sun infused-flower essences

6 pints (3 liters) fresh pure water or distilled water

4 handfuls freshly picked flowers specific to the malady being treated (see page 106)

organic brandy or vodka, at least 40% proof

Serves 6

For centuries, flower essences have been used to heal many infirmities (see page 106). While the health-food store versions are handy, they are also very expensive. You can make your own flower essences at home. Start by making a mother tincture—the most concentrated form of the essence—which can then be used to make stock bottles. The stock bottles are used to make dosage bottles for the most diluted form of the essence, which is the one you actually take.

Ideally, begin early in the morning, by picking your chosen flowers by 9 am at the latest. This leaves you with 3 hours of sunlight before the noon hour, after which the sunlight is less effective, even draining.

Put the water in a large glass mixing bowl. To avoid touching the flowers, place them carefully on the surface of the water using tweezers or chopsticks, until the surface is covered. Leave the bowl in the sun for 3–4 hours, or until the flowers begin to fade.

Now, delicately remove the flowers, being careful not to touch the water. Strain the flower essence water through cheesecloth (muslin) into a large pitcher. Half-fill a green or blue 8 oz. (230 ml) sealable glass bottle with the flower essence water, and top up with the brandy or vodka (this will extend the shelf life of your flower water to 3 months if stored in a cool, dark cupboard). This is your mother tincture: Label it with the date and the name of the flower. Use any remaining essence water to water the flowers you've been working with, and murmur a prayer of gratitude for their beauty and healing power.

To make a stock bottle from your mother tincture, fill a 1 oz. (30 ml) dropper bottle three-quarters full of brandy, top up with spring water, then add 3 drops of the mother tincture. This will last at least 3 months and enable you to make lots of dosage bottles.

To make a dosage bottle for any flower essence, just add 2 or 3 drops of the stock bottle to another 1 oz. (30 ml) dropper bottle one-quarter full of brandy and three-quarters full of distilled water. Anytime you need some of this gentle medicine, place 4 drops from the dosage bottle under your tongue or add it to a glass of water. Take or sip four times a day, or as often as you feel the need. You can't overdose on flower remedies, but more frequent, rather than larger, doses are much more effective.

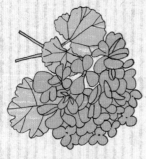

Flower essence remedies

One drop from a dosage bottle of flower essence mixed with 1 oz. (30 ml) distilled water can also be used to remedy the following:

- *Addiction:* agrimony, skullcap
- *Anger:* blue flag, chamomile, nettle
- *Anxiety:* aspen, garlic, gentian, lemon balm, periwinkle, rosemary, white chestnut
- *Bereavement:* honeysuckle
- *Depression:* black cohosh, borage, chamomile, geranium, larch, lavender, mustard, sunflower, yerba santa
- *Exhaustion:* aloe, olive, sweet chestnut, yarrow
- *Fear:* basil, datura, ginger, mallow, peony, poppy, water lily
- *Heartbreak:* borage, hawthorn, heartsease
- *Lethargy:* aloe, peppermint, thyme
- *Spiritual blocks:* ginseng, lady's slipper, oak
- *Stress:* dill, echinacea, lemon balm, mistletoe, thyme

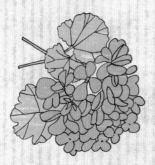

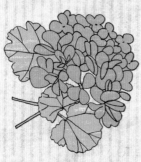

Imbued with love

Lavender- and rosemary-infused vodka

Vodka is easily infused with the flavor of flowers, herbs, fruit, and even vegetables. Try this combination of lavender, to calm and heal, and rosemary, to dispel negative spirits. Both of these are love herbs. What could be better? When you've finished infusing the vodka, tie the dried herbs into a bundle with string and use them when you next make a fire in the hearth. The scented smoke will imbue your home with coziness, calm, healing, and love.

- ❖ 2 sprigs fresh rosemary
- ❖ 3 sprigs fresh lavender
- ❖ 2 pint (1 liter) bottle of vodka

Rinse the herbs in cool water and gently pat them dry. Put them in a sterilized 2 pint (1 liter) Mason jar (see box below), pour in vodka to cover the herbs to the top, and seal tightly. Shake vigorously and place in your pantry or a dark closet, making sure to shake it at least once a day. After 2 days, take a spoon and taste the vodka. If the taste suits you, go ahead and strain the herbs out using cheesecloth (muslin) or a paper coffee filter. Otherwise leave it another day, up to a maximum of 5 days in total. Set the herbs aside and leave them to dry. Pour the strained vodka into a bottle, and label it with its name and the date. Your infused vodka will taste wonderful served ice-cold and neat. To your health!

sterilizing your canning jars

Wash the jars in hot soapy water and rinse in scalding water, or use a dishwasher on the hottest setting. Place the jars on a rack set in a deep pot and cover with hot water. Bring the water to a boil and boil the canning jars, covered, for 15 minutes. Using jar tongs, carefully remove the jars, empty out any hot water, and sit them upside down on a clean, dry towel. Once dry, they are ready to fill with your potions and produce!

Apple brandy spirits

- ❖ 4 sweet dessert apples
- ❖ 2 cups (450 ml) brandy
- ❖ 2 cups (450 ml) vodka

This delightfully easy recipe will produce a flavorful homemade liqueur that smells as good as it tastes. If you are interested in making a hassle-free bottle of spirits, apples are a wonderful way to start.

Peel, core, and slice the apples. Place the slices in a sterilized 2 pint (1 liter) Mason jar (see box on page 107), and pour in the brandy and vodka to cover. Put the jar in a cool, dark place, such as your pantry or a closet. Leave to infuse for a month or so, or until it is to your taste. The combination of sweet apples and brandy gives a luscious fruity flavor, with no need for sugar. When it is infused to your satisfaction, use a strainer (sieve) to filter the liqueur. Pour into a pretty, sealable bottle and enjoy at your next pagan party.

APPLES EVERYWHERE
Apples can be used in this way with any spirit, so let your imagination run wild!

Longevity liqueur
Homemade pear elixir

- ❖ 2 cardamom pods
- ❖ 3 large ripe pears
- ❖ 2 in. (5 cm) piece of lemon peel
- ❖ 2 pints (1 liter) vodka

Pears have long been prized in Asia for being a lucky fruit that also offers a long and prosperous life. The great magical teacher Scott Cunningham advocated their use in love spells. This pear liqueur is a special brew indeed.

Sterilize a 2 pint (1 liter) Mason jar with a lid, preferably a dark-colored one if you can find it (see box on page 107).

Crush the cardamom pods and set aside. Peel and core the pears and cut into thin slices. Gently place the pears in the jar. Put the crushed cardamom and lemon peel on top, and cover all with the vodka, leaving a gap of 1 in. (2.5 cm) at the top. Close the jar and tighten the lid, then gently shake it twice. Store it in a cool, dark cupboard or closet for 10 days. When the time is up, pour the contents into a mixing bowl and mash thoroughly using the back of a fork or a potato masher. Strain the mixture into another bowl, using a colander lined with a paper coffee filter or cheesecloth (muslin). Repeat this process twice, then pour the pear liqueur back into a sterilized Mason jar. If you're feeling fancy, store the liqueur in a pretty bottle, but make sure it is sterilized and tightly sealed. Live long and prosper!

Herbal infusion invocation

For any witch, the kitchen is the laboratory for alchemy. The transference of the pure essence of an herb into oil or liqueur is nothing less than magic. Adding the following step to the process of infusing honors its alchemical aspect and adds enchantment to the final product. After you have bottled up your infusions, and before you store them in a dark pantry, place them on your altar. Check your almanac (see Resources, page 140) to see what sign the sun and moon are in, and what the moon phase is. Have a pretty label and a colored pen at the ready. Light a green candle, hold one of the bottles in both hands, and pray aloud:

Under this moon and sun.

Green magic binds into one.

By my hand. I filled this bottle with grace.

To bring enjoyment to all who come to this place.

Blessings for all: and so be it.

Take the pen and write on the label the kind of herbal oil you have made (see example, right).

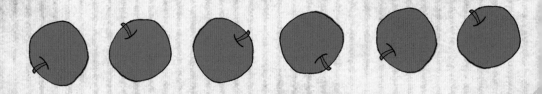

Apple Brandy Spirits
Made on June 15, under the Gemini Sun and Taurus New Moon

Astrological herbology

You can also choose the herbs for your altar based on your sun or moon sign. Explore making tinctures, incense, oils, potpourri, and other magical potions for your rituals using celestial correspondences. For example, if the new moon is in Aries when you are performing an attraction ritual, try using peppermint or fennel, two herbs that are sacred to the sign of the ram. If you are creating a special altar for the time when the sun is in the sign of Cancer, use incense oils, teas, and herbs that correspond to that astrological energy, such as jasmine and lemon. These correspondences create a synthesis of energy that adds to the effectiveness of your magical work. There is information on this elsewhere in this book and also in *The Book of Kitchen Witchery*, a book I loved writing. Further references for keeping track of moon signs and phases are included in the Resources (see page 140). Keep notes in your Book of Shadows on what works best for you.

Aries, ruled by Mars: carnation, cedar wood, clove, cumin, fennel, juniper, peppermint, pine

Taurus, ruled by Venus: apple, daisy, lilac, magnolia, oak moss, orchid, plumeria, rose, thyme, tonka bean, vanilla, violet

Gemini, ruled by Mercury: bergamot, clover, dill, lavender, lemongrass, lily, mint, parsley

Cancer, ruled by the moon: eucalyptus, gardenia, jasmine, lemon, lotus, myrrh, rose, sandalwood

Leo, ruled by the sun: acacia, cinnamon, heliotrope, nutmeg, orange, rosemary

Virgo, ruled by Mercury: almond, bergamot, cypress, mace, mint, moss, patchouli

Libra, ruled by Venus: catnip, marjoram, mugwort, spearmint, sweet pea, thyme, vanilla

Scorpio, ruled by Pluto: allspice, basil, cumin, galangal, ginger

Sagittarius, ruled by Jupiter: anise, cedar wood, honeysuckle, sassafras, star anise

Capricorn, ruled by Saturn: mimosa, vervain, vetiver

Aquarius, ruled by Uranus: acacia, almond, citron, cypress, lavender, mimosa, peppermint, pine

Pisces, ruled by Neptune: anise, catnip, clove, gardenia, lemon, orris, sarsaparilla, sweet pea

Preserves and pickles

One of the lasting joys of gardening is "putting up" or preserving your harvest. It does require work, but the payoff will be a pantry full of fine-looking jars filled with delicious produce that will feed your family and friends for months to come. It has been very gratifying—albeit amusing—to see the homey art of pickling become a hipster hobby. May this trend of preserving homegrown food never end! It is also a wonderful way to instill enchantment, the energy of abundance, and healing magic into your family's food.

The enchanted orchard

We often think of herbs and flowers as having magical properties, but it is much less commonly known that fruit also contains much magic that you must try for yourself.

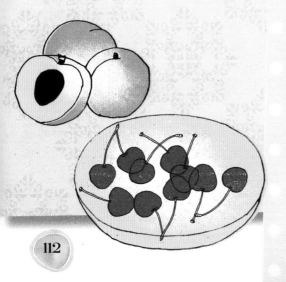

Fruits of love

Apricot: This juicy treasure is associated with Venus and the power of love, and it is believed that drinking the nectar will make you more appealing romantically. The juice of the apricot is used in rituals and love potions. It is truly a food of the goddess!

Avocado: The lusciousness of the avocado is not just delicious, it also brings forth beauty and lust.

Cherry: Beloved for their bright red color and fabulously sweet taste, cherries are associated with romance as well as powers of divination. They are useful in love spells. The Japanese believe that tying a strand of your hair to the blossom of a cherry tree will bring you a lover.

Orange: Like the joyful color of this fruit, oranges are a fruit of happiness in love and marriage. Dried blossoms added to a hot bath make you more beautiful. A spritz of orange juice will enhance the potency of any love potion. Orange sachets and other gifts containing this fruit offer felicity, so it is an ideal gift for newlyweds.

Fruits of abundance

Banana: A bunch of bananas packs a magical punch with powers of abundance and fertility for both men and women. Anyone who gets married beneath a banana-tree bower will have a lucky marriage. One caveat, though: Never cut a banana, only break it apart. Otherwise, you'll bring bad luck to your household.

Grape: Planting grapevines grants you the ability to make money magic happen, as well as blessing gardening and farming: The ancient Romans painted pictures of grapes on the garden walls to ensure a good harvest and fertility for women. Magical spell workings for money are abetted greatly by placing a bowl of grapes on the altar. For mental focus during a busy day, eat some grapes.

Lemon: This beloved member of the citrus family confers the rare power of longevity, as well as those of faithful friendship, purification, love, and luck. Lemon juice mixed with water can be used to consecrate magical tools and other objects during the full moon. Dried lemon flowers and peel can be used in love potions and sachets. Bake a lemon pie for the object of your desire, and he or she will remain faithful to you for all time. Imbibing lemon-leaf tea, on the other hand, stirs lust.

Pear: It is believed that this intriguingly shaped fruit brings prosperity and long life. Somewhat similarly to the peach (see page 114), the pear has powers of lust and love. Shared with a partner, a pear can be used to induce sexual arousal. Pear wood is also very good for magical wands.

Pineapple: This is renowned as the symbol of hospitality, and represents neighborliness, abundance, and chastity. Dried pineapple in a sachet added to bathwater will bring great luck. The juice encourages moderation and prevents you from rash impulsiveness in romance. The dried peel is great in money spells and mixtures.

Pomegranate: This most beautiful of fruits gives powers of divination, making wishes come true and engendering wealth. Eating the seeds can increase fruitfulness in childbearing; you can also carry the rind in a sachet in your pocket if you are looking to have a child. Always make a wish before eating the fruit, for that wish will come true.

Tomato: A reminder that the tomato is a fruit! An easy money spell is to place a fresh-off-the-vine tomato on the mantelpiece every few days to bring prosperity. Eating tomatoes inspires love. They are also useful in the garden for warding off pests of all kinds.

Fruits for protection:

Blackberry: Thorny blackberry vines are wonderful as protection around your home and in wreaths for your front door. Blackberries are the medicine that pops up everywhere, offering a delightful snack and serious healing, love, and abundance. Both the vine and the berries can be used for money-bringing spells.

Blueberry: Of all the fruits of the vine, blueberries offer the greatest protection. Rub a drop of blueberry juice under the welcome mat at the threshold of your front door to ward off bad energy and evil if you feel someone is attempting to do you harm with hexes or sending bad energy your way.

Fig: Wherever it is grown, a fig tree will bring good luck and safety. Figs have held a place in our culture since the story of Adam and Eve in the Garden of Eden. Unsurprisingly, they are associated with sexuality and fecundity. If eaten ripe off the tree, this fruit will aid in conception and help with impotence. A fig tree grown outside the bedroom will bring deeply restful sleep and prophetic dreams. Outside your kitchen, a fig tree will ensure that there is always plenty of food for your family. A folk charm claims that gifting someone a fig grown by your own hand binds them to you—so wield your figs wisely.

Peach: An amulet made with a peach pit (stone) can ward off evil. A fallen branch from a peach tree can make an excellent magical wand, while a piece of its wood carried in your pocket is an excellent talisman for a long life. It might seem obvious, but eating peaches encourages love. They also enhance wisdom.

Plum: Plums are for protection and add sweetness to romantic love. A fallen branch from a plum tree over the door keeps out negative energy and wards off evil.

Raspberry: This sweet berry has tremendous powers over true love and the safety of your home. Hang the vines at doors when a person in the house has died so that the spirit won't enter the home again. Raspberry leaves are carried by pregnant women to help with the pains of childbirth and even pregnancy itself. Raspberries are often served to induce love. (Strawberry leaves also help with childbirth, and the leaves are also carried for luck.)

farmers' market potpourri

Even if you don't have a citrus orchard out back, you can still make your own home-freshening mix of potpourri. Increase the benefits of this glorious fruit by making lemonade, limeade, or orange juice, then slice up the remainder of the fruit. Lay the rind and slices on a large baking sheet, and leave to dry for 3 days. Add dried rose petals, bunches of dried lavender and rosemary, or mint for a wonderfully fresh scent. Tuck into cheesecloth (muslin) bags, tie up with a pretty, colorful ribbon, and you have a lovely all-occasion gift for housewarmings and holidays. It is truly a blessing for any home.

Ingredients

- 5 cups (1 kg) strawberries, hulled
- 1 tsp sweet (unsalted) butter
- 1¾ oz. powdered fruit pectin
- 7 cups (1.4 kg) granulated sugar
- ½ cup (40 g) fresh basil, chopped

Makes 3 pints (1.4 liters)

Love and money
Strawberry jam

July is one of the sweetest times to enjoy your garden, and strawberries are a harbinger of the good summery times ahead. They are also widely regarded as an aphrodisiac. Basil, meanwhile, brings money to your house. This lucky jam will be a great gift to your household, and to anyone who is served it.

Crush the strawberries gently in a big bowl using the back of a large spoon or a potato masher. Melt the butter in a large pot over a gentle heat, and pour in the crushed strawberries. Stir in the powdered pectin. Bring the mixture to a boil over a high heat, stirring constantly. Add the sugar and bring back to a rolling boil. Boil, stirring constantly, for 1 minute. Add the chopped basil.

Remove the pot from the heat and skim off any foam using a slotted spoon. Ladle the hot mixture into six sterilized ½ pint (280 ml) canning jars (see box on page 107), leaving ¼ in. (5 mm) at the top. Remove any air bubbles by tamping down the jam with the underneath of a sterilized metal spoon. Add more hot jam if necessary to bring it back up to the original level. Wipe the rims of the jars carefully, then seal, label, and store the jars (see box opposite). This Love and Money jam is so sweet and so effective, you'll run out long before a year goes by!

sealing and storing homemade preserves

It is important to ensure your jam jars are sealed correctly. Once you have decanted jam or placed pickles and brining liquid into your sterilized jars, screw the lids on firmly. Place them in a large pot of simmering water, ensuring they are covered with at least 1 in. (2.5 cm) water. Bring to a boil and simmer for 10 minutes. Using jar tongs, lift the jars out and stand them upright on a clean towel to cool at room temperature. You will hear the lids seal when they make a popping noise as the domed lid is sucked down. Let them sit undisturbed for 12 hours, then check for proper seals by pressing the middle of the lid with your finger. If the lid springs back up, it is not sealed. (Any jars that fail to seal can be refrigerated and must be enjoyed within 4 weeks, unless otherwise stated in the recipe.) Store the jars in a cool, dark place. The preserves will last for up to a year.

SMALLER BATCHES
If you're making a smaller quantity of preserve, or perhaps decanting into smaller jars as gifts, you do not need to seal the jars—simply pour the preserve into sterilized jars and then refrigerate them. However, they will only last for 4 weeks, so will need to be eaten up quickly!

Blessed be
Blackberry jam

- ❖ 2 cups (400 g) blackberries (or try raspberries or strawberries)
- ❖ 2 cups (400 g) granulated sugar
- ❖ 2 tsp lemon juice
- ❖ 1 slice lemon rind
- ❖ 1 slice apple

Makes 2 pints (1 liter)

This is a tried-and-true recipe for a simple berry jam. Our family favorite is blackberries, since the color is nearly as delicious as the taste. Berries contain protection magic as well as that of abundance, and according to folklore, vampires are afraid of blackberry vines. The jam is fabulous spread on toasted Cheesy Beer Loaf (see page 98).

Crush the berries gently in a large bowl with the back of a spoon or a potato masher. Place all the ingredients in a large pot and boil over a high heat for 5 minutes, stirring the mixture to prevent it from sticking or burning. Reduce the heat to medium-high and continue to boil and stir. Remove any foam with a large spoon. After a half hour, the jam will begin to thicken. If it is setting too slowly, add more lemon juice or another slice of apple. (Pectin, which is regularly used to thicken jams and jellies, is made from apples, so a slice of apple will serve the same purpose.)

When the jam has reached your preferred thickness, pour it into sterilized ½ pint (280 ml) jars (see box on page 107). The jars should be warm when the jam is added, so keep them in the oven, dishwasher, or water bath after sterilizing, until you need them; the same goes for the lids and rings. Make sure to leave a good ½ in. (1 cm) gap between the jam and the top of the jar. Screw the lids on firmly, then seal, label, and store the jars (see box on page 117).

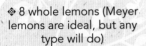

Sunshine in a bottle
Canned lemon curd

- ❖ 8 whole lemons (Meyer lemons are ideal, but any type will do)
- ❖ 2½ cups (500 g) granulated sugar
- ❖ 2 cups (450 g) sweet (unsalted) butter
- ❖ 8 eggs, beaten

Makes 4 pints (2 liters)

We all know the adage, "when life gives you lemons …," but I would update this classic with the suggestion to make lemon curd! With just four ingredients, it is not a complex chore but a delightful way to take your bounty of citrus and create a sweet and creamy joy-filled treat for you and your loved ones to enjoy for months to come.

Sterilize 8 clean glass jars (ideally ½ pint/250 ml Mason jars; see box on page 107).

Grate the lemon zest into a medium pan. Squeeze every drop of the juice from the lemons into a bowl—you should have about 1½ cups (330 ml). Add the juice to the pan, along with the sugar. Cut the butter into small pieces and add it to the pan gradually.

Place the pan over a low heat, and stir until the butter has melted and the sugar dissolves. Strain the beaten eggs through a fine strainer (sieve) into the pan. Cook on a medium heat for 10–15 minutes, stirring frequently. As it heats up, the mixture will begin to thicken and take on a creamy consistency.

When the lemon sauce is thick enough to coat the back of the spoon, remove the pan from the heat. Fill the jars with the lemon curd to within ⅛ in. (3 mm) of the rims. Carefully wipe the rims clean and top with the hot lids. If you are using Mason jars, screw the bands down until they are finger tight, then seal, label, and store the jars (see box on page 117)

Your garden in a jar Pride of pantry pickles

- ❖ 3 dozen cucumbers (3–4 in./7–10 cm long)
- ❖ 3 cups (675 ml) white vinegar
- ❖ 3 cups (675 ml) water
- ❖ 6 tbsp Kosher salt to season (per jar)
- ❖ ½–1 clove of garlic, sliced
- ❖ ½ tbsp mustard seeds
- ❖ 1 bunch fresh dill or ½ tsp dried dill (you can use the seed heads, leaves, and stems, too)

My mother was very proud of her pickles. This recipe was handed down from generation to generation in our family, and it can also be used to pickle almost any other vegetable you fancy, including onions, bell peppers, squash, baby corn, green tomatoes, and cauliflower. Using your own homegrown dill is a wonderful finishing touch. For this recipe, use three 2 pint (1 liter) Mason jars or six 1 pint (0.5 liter) jars.

Wash the cucumbers in cool water. Pour the vinegar, water, and Kosher salt into a large stockpot and bring to a boil. This is the brining liquid. Sterilize the jars (see box on page 107), then place the garlic, mustard seeds, and half the dill in the bottom of each. Pack the cucumbers vertically into the jar until it is half-full, then add the rest of the dill. Fill the jar to the top with cucumbers, leaving ½ in. (1 cm) at the top for brine. After you have poured in the brining liquid, seal the jars (see box on page 117). Label your pickle jars and store them on a cool, dark shelf for up to 2 weeks.

the magical correspondences of pickling

Pickling is not just about preserving the delectable taste of your herbs and vegetables, but also about bottling their magical powers. You can quite consciously design a meal to conjure a peaceful household or to attract more money, love, or luck into your life. Time to get creative! This recipe alone has the following associations:

- *Cucumber:* healing, peace
- *Dill:* prosperity, safety, luck
- *Garlic:* protection, healing
- *Salt:* purification
- *Vinegar:* security, cleansing

PICKLED VEGETABLE POWERS

- *Beans:* protection from evil spirits
- *Beets:* love spells
- *Celery:* psychic powers
- *Corn:* divination, luck
- *Lemon:* purification, longevity, friendship
- *Olives:* healing peace, potency
- *Onions:* protection, healing, dreams
- *Potatoes:* healing magic
- *Zucchini (courgettes):* prosperity

CHAPTER 7

Domestic Deities *and* Guardian Gods

Lunar Lore, Astrological Aspects,
and Spiritual Correspondences
to Use in Your Spell Work

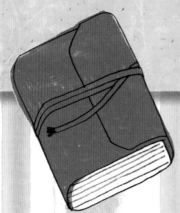

Working with the celestial elements—from gods and goddesses to ancient symbols and sigils, to accessing the eternal wisdom of the sun, moon, and stars in the sky—is some of the deepest magic you can apply. When you synchronize your life with the phases of the moon, the cycle of astrological signs, and the divinities who rule each planet and sign, you will be aligning with the Wheel of the Year, living in harmony with the celestial sphere. This can happen fairly quickly, too. By tracking it through making notes in your Book of Shadows, you'll start to notice when your spells are most successful and begin to increase your prowess in the craft. This will enable you to design your own rituals for house magic, based on the correspondences that are most effective in your spell work. Discover the gods and goddesses that you feel most connected to, and invoke them. Find which moon sign boosts the power of your conjuring. Discover your personal power phase. The tools and secrets revealed in this chapter will enable you to live a sacred and magical life every day of the year.

Designing your own home and garden rituals

Drawing on the power of the earth, you can perform ceremonies of immense strength and richness to further your personal and spiritual goals. You can begin new projects, deepen your dreams, and ground yourself in nature. You can plant a magical garden with seeds of change. You can sculpt or carve a wooden or stone goddess for your altar. You can cook a sacred meal to serve after ritual work. You can perform rituals outdoors, celebrating the beauty of our planet—a gift we all share and must preserve.

Other earth elemental rites that you can design on your own could include ceremonies for fertility, bodily health and strength, prosperity, property, success, and manifestation. There is no exact science to writing rituals; through practice, it will become an art for you. Match the words and correspondences to your intention, and you will be a creator of rituals. It is natural that once you are completely comfortable working with the realm of existing rituals, you should begin to trust your own intuition and create your own. Listen to your inner voice, trust yourself, and refer to your Book of Shadows for which signs of the sun and moon, as well as which herbs, crystals, herbs, and essential oils, are best for you.

Correspondences are a start, but you must take a leap of faith and delve into the depths of your being for rituals to create, enact, and share with the world. Start with the affirmative changes you wish to make in your home by giving thought to your intention and picking what corresponds with it. Let's say you are going to start working from home. Begin with the Buckets of Money Floor Wash from Chapter Two and clear the way for positive new energy. You will want colors, crystals, herbs, figurines, and other elements that will bring mental clarity, abundance, efficiency, and good luck to your home office, and you might want to consider an office altar or shrine featuring yellow quartz or jade with green candles in a gold-colored candleholder, and to have a potted palm by your desk with a statue of the hunting goddess Artemis, bringer of luck. Take out your Book of Shadows and meditate on your magical intention, then begin writing the words of the spell that will create success for you in your new home office. Follow your intuition: Use it as your rudder and your guide.

When you undertake your own spell work, you can draw on the wealth of the world's mythologies and create original rites based on the merging of your own intention and the deity's domain. When you call on the gods and goddesses in your Wiccan circles and ceremonies, you will need to have an understanding of their realms—know thy divinity. You should feel drawn to whomever you invoke. If you feel inclined toward a certain deity, do your homework and find out everything you can about them.

Discretion and caution should be exercised anytime you call for the aid of celestial beings. Kali, for example, is a dark goddess associated with destruction, and should never be invoked for love and harmony. Similarly, Mars is the god of war and would not be called into a peace ritual. You can use the power of the gods and goddesses in very practical ways. A dear friend of mine who was recently laid off in a corporate restructuring researched the rites of Artemis, who brings fast luck. A man looking for physical love, on the other hand, could invoke the lusty Arcadian pipe-playing god Pan.

I strongly advise employing common sense and excellent manners in any dealings with deities and denizens of the mythical realm. The friendship of fairies can be a blessing and a curse. If you call on the fairy folk and don't expressly thank them for their aid, they may play tricks on you and make mischief in many ways. If your car keys go missing after you have invoked the fairies, you know you have been insufficiently courteous.

Domestic goddesses

A form of magic handed down from antiquity is to have a domestic goddess figure in your home; archeologists have found them among the most ancient artifacts. It is a wonderful energy generator to have such a figurine decorating your home altar. It is very important to choose the divinity with whom you feel the deepest connection when invoking her for house magic.

Goddesses of protection

Agnayi: For people on the Indian subcontinent, she is the equivalent of Vesta as a domestic fire goddess. She is invoked for protection, and especially for the safekeeping of children.

The Eye Goddess: This most ancient of Mediterranean deities is depicted as an all-seeing eye, and represents justice. No transgression can be hidden from her. Dating back to 3500 BCE, she is often depicted as a single, unblinking eye. Anytime you need the truth brought to light, call her up. She also offers protection from thieves if you hang her eye in your windows, and she is an excellent resident in your magical kitchen. She is often mistaken for the "evil eye," but is a benevolent presence who will watch out for you and yours 24/7.

Aradia: The Italian "Queen of the Witches" and protector of women; originally a rustic moon goddess from Tuscany. Aradia can help to keep vampires away, including "energy vampires," people who—often unknowingly—steal and take up your personal energy.

Juno: The Romans depended on this generous presence to watch over the daughters of the earth she is regarded as the mother of all women and can be invoked for any magical gathering of women. Her special domain is as a protector of brides. When preparing feasts and cakes for weddings, ask Juno to bring her brightest blessin,

Brigid: This Celtic solar goddess of poetry, smithcraft, and healing existed long before the Catholic Church adopted her and canonized her as saint. She is a protector of animals and childre Brigid can be invoked to bless your kitchen tools Your pots, pans, and knives can all have the streng of this bright being, forged by the fire of the sur

Ashnan: The Sumerian grain goddess and protector of the fields is depicted in ancient Babylonian imagery as a beautiful young woman handing worshipful men a single stalk of grain.

Bast: Egypt's cat goddess protected the lands. Bast also has childbirth, healing, passion, pleasure, happiness, and, of course, cats in her sphere of influence. She can come into your life in the form of a stray cat—a familiar—and can become a real guardian for your hearth and home.

conjuring the ancients: symbol writing

If you wish to make direct contact with a deity, here is a way to see through the veil between the worlds. At any herbal store or metaphysical shop, obtain 2 tbsp each of dried mugwort, mint, rosemary, and, if you can get it, wormwood. (Dried magical herbs often come in mini bags that contain 1 tbsp each.) The last is a bit harder to come by, but worth the effort. Crumble the herbs between your hands gently until they are ground to a fine consistency, and put them in a baking pan (tray). Make sure the crumbled herb dust is spread evenly over the pan.

Light yellow candles and close your eyes. With the forefinger of your left hand, touch the center of the pan. Run your finger back and forth in a completely random pattern—don't think, just rely on your instincts—for 2 minutes. Open your eyes, look at the pattern you have drawn, and write down what the symbols and designs bring to mind. Also write down the thoughts you were having while you were drawing. You will receive a message from your god or goddess. It might be in the form of a picture. For example, a cat shape would indicate that your message comes from the cat goddess Bast, ruler of pregnancy and childbirth, and of protection. It may also mean that a stray cat might show up as your personal guardian, which is a great gift from Bast.

Goddesses of inspiration

Sige: This gnostic goddess charges us to be silent. In Roman mythology she stands for the secret name of Rome, which could not be spoken aloud, and thus she is depicted as a hooded woman with her finger on her lips. Gnostic texts speak of Sige's origins as the mother of Sophia. She is the primordial female creator: Out of silence came the *logos*, or word. The cult, rituals, and folklore regarding Sige were held so strictly secret that we know nothing about them now. However, since creation comes out of silence, you have complete creative freedom to make new myths, stories, and celebrations for this obscure deity. Silent celebrations, quiet meditations, and secret spells would no doubt gain her approval.

Persephone: The daughter of Demeter, Persephone is bidden to spend half her time in the underworld with her husband, Hades. She is a harbinger of change as she rises from the dark world after winter, bringing spring and the growing season with her. The pomegranate is her signifier. Invoke her for rites of spring.

Artemis: The huntress or woman warrior travels with a pack of devoted dogs and can be called on in times of need or to bring fast luck. The goddess of the hunt is also the ruler of the moon, and can be invoked for lunar magic. Call her to aid you anytime you are looking for something. She can represent the earth element on your house altar.

Goddesses of life and creation

Gaia: This Greek deity is seen as the mother of all life—and sometimes called Mother Nature. Born at the dawn of creation, she personifies the Earth, and as such can represent the earth element in your rituals.

Hathor: This "cow goddess" represents life, and was beloved in ancient Egypt for her ability to bring fertility. She was also associated with royalty, and her priests were artists, dancers, trained midwives, and seers. As the celestial cow, she held the golden disk of the sun between her horns. Hathor's other sacred animals include the lion, cobra, falcon, and hippopotamus. The sacred sistrum, a rattle used in ritual, was used to summon her. Mirrors were also her sacred tool. During spring rains and floods, you can stage a ritual dance for her to sanctify the joy of life and bless your newly planted garden.

Sunna: This ancient Germanic goddess of the sun is proof that our big star is not always deified as male. The Teutons also referred to this very important divine entity as "Glory of Elves." In the great northern European saga the Poetic Edda, Sunna was said to have a daughter who shed light on a brand-new world. Other sun goddesses include the Arabian Attar, the Japanese Amaterasu, and the British Celtic Sulis, "the sun's eye."

Isis: Isis was the only goddess who could guarantee the immortality of the Egyptian pharaohs, resurrecting them as she did Osiris. Worship of her spread, and became an enormous cult that appealed to the Greeks, the Romans, and throughout the Hellenic world. She is the daughter of Nuit, goddess of the sky, and Seb, god of earth, and has great appeal as a divine mother. The ancients worshiped her as the Queen of Heaven, and she is often depicted with wings. She is the link between birth and death, and can be invoked in rituals designed to celebrate existence under our banner of stars. She is typically depicted as a beautiful winged woman, crowned with the disk of the sun gleaming golden. The palm tree is sacred to Isis and can be used in ritual. You can lay palm leaves in your path and walk in procession. The palm has been used ritually in various ways throughout the world (see box below).

Venus: The Roman goddess of love is associated with ultimate femininity, ultimate sexuality, ultimate fertility, and all that is beautiful. The word venerate means to worship Venus, and she should be venerated in all the love spells of your own design as well as celebrations and circles taking place on her day (Friday). The lore and mythology of Venus are well known, since she was imprinted on our consciousness by the early Renaissance artist Botticelli as a beautiful naked nymph rising on a half-shell from the foamy wave of the ocean. Honor her by creating dances on the beach that are celebratory of womanhood, and write love prayers and poems inspired by the love in your own heart.

Woman of Willendorf Sometimes called the Venus of Willendorf, this Paleolithic northern European deity predates the traditional Venus— she dates back to 25,000 BCE—and represents abundance and female strength. Her appealing, ample shape represents fertility and the feminine, and she can also represent the element of earth on your house altar.

protective palm-tree house magic

- In Cuba, people sweep one another with palm branches that have been blessed with holy water in order to keep them safe from evil spirits.

- Puerto Ricans weave palm leaves into crosses and use them as protective amulets. They also hang the crosses in their homes to encourage abundance and to keep the home sacred.

- In Belgium, sections of palms are kept in the fields to ensure a copious harvest.

- The French decorate the graves of beloved relatives with palm leaves that have been especially blessed for that purpose.

- The people of New Orleans plant palmetto palms beside a fountain or pond on their property to bring money, love, luck, and good health.

Goddesses of wisdom

Athena: The goddess of wisdom, who also rules over battle. Call on her to help resolve any disagreements. Under her domain is the owl, and also olive trees. She stopped wars in ancient times with offerings of an olive branch.

Shekina: The female deity who is "God's glory" and the consort of the Hebrew god Yahweh. Older rabbinical texts describe her as the "splendor that feeds angels." She was the only one to get away with being angry with Yahweh. In gnosticism, she is associated with Sophia, whose name means "wisdom" in Greek; she comes through in *logos*, or the Holy Word, and is the first emanation of the Shekina. These ancient divinities came to be represented by Mary Magdalene, the companion of God's son, Jesus Christ. Having been redacted from all biblical texts, Shekina was veiled in obscurity until medieval cabalists rediscovered her. Glimmers of her presence show up in passages of the Talmud that tell the story of the exiled Israelis wandering into the wilderness with Joseph's bones and a second ossuary, or "bone box," containing "the Shekina" in the form of a pair of stone tablets. Be creative in designing rituals, altars, offerings, and ceremonies honoring this deity, since you are rebuilding a lost part of goddess history. One daring ritual could include convening a women's circle and rewriting the tablets of wisdom. Call upon your inner Sophia and inner knowledge for guidance in this highly original approach to ritual.

Cerridwen: I was named in honor of this aspect of the Triple Goddess, she of deep elder wisdom. In Welsh legend, Cerridwen represents the crone, the darker aspect of the goddess. She has powers of prophecy, and is the keeper of the cauldron of knowledge and inspiration in the Underworld. She is a mother goddess who makes sure to feed her followers and minds the fields.

Selene: She is the full moon, another Greek aspect of the lunation cycle. She sheds light on the world and on us all, inside and out. Her mythology is that, as a teacher of magic and all things supernatural, she passed her special knowledge on to her students. She is also a mentor, and her light illuminates our intelligence and ability to think clearly and logically.

Guardian gods

Invoking the energy of a god can infuse your ritual work with great power. The panoply of pagan divinities described here can be called upon as protectors of your home, your property, your family, and your creative projects. What do you need? Ask for help and your guardian god will come to you.

For example, I invoked Apollo who is a helpmate to writers when writing this book. As a result, I felt more connected to divine energy and inspiration and words came more easily to me. Similarly, a couple of years ago, I feared for my garden because of a prolonged drought, and summoned the aid of the Green Man with a shrine and regular prayers. After a fortnight, the rain fell, and my garden survived the drought. What's more, I stored water from that rainfall in a barrel, so that one storm sustained my garden for months afterward. Thank the gods!

Gods of protection

Thor—Sky and Thunder: The Norse god of justice and battle uses his thunderbolt to exact his will. Medieval Scandinavians believed the crack of lightning and thunder was Thor's chariot rolling through the heavens. Turn to him when you need spirituality to solve a legal matter. He is also a powerful protection deity to use in ritual.

Mithra—Bringer of Light: This Persian god of the sun and protector of warriors corresponds with the element of air and comes from a deep mysterious tradition of Mesopotamian magic and fertility rites. If you have a loved one in a war far from home, create a special altar for your beloved with Mithra, who is the soldiers' god.

Gods of vitality and power

Cernunnos—The Green Man: Also known as Herne the Hunter, Cernunnos is the Horned God of the Celts and embodies the virility and spirit of the wild man. He is also one to invoke for any kind of animal magic. Couples hoping to increase fertility, or a vintner or cultivator desirous of a more abundant crop, can call on this spirit of fecundity. You can symbolize the energy of Cernunnos and represent the element of earth with antlers on your kitchen altar or a Green Man statue on your outdoor altar.

Adonis—Gardeners' Guardian: As we all know, Adonis is the god of love and partner to the goddess of love, Aphrodite. What is less well known about this gorgeous being is that he is also an herbal deity with dominion over certain plants and flowers, has the power of earth and fertility, and is a guardian of health. While Adonis is often called upon for love rites and spells, he can also be invoked for help with the environment, and you should invite him to watch over your herb and vegetable patch. A lovely invitation to this garden god is to put a little statue of a handsome male deity at the front of your plot and lay an offering of flowers at his feet. I have no doubt that your garden will grow very well soon after!

Lugh—Guardian of the Harvest: The "Shining One" of Celtic mythology, Lugh is the warrior sun god and also guardian of crops. Lughnasa, which takes place at the beginning of August, is a festival in honor of the harvest god. At the end of summer and the beginning of fall (autumn), Wiccans should hold rituals of gratitude for the abundance of the crop and the gift that is life. This will keep the flow of prosperity coming to you and yours. Lugh also has dominion over late summer storms, so anyone experiencing drought or wildfires can pray to him for rain.

Dagon—God of Loaves and Fishes: The first incarnation of Dagon was as a corn and grain divinity. The Phoenicians embraced him as a god of great importance representing death and rebirth, depicted as half-fish and half-man. He was said to give power to oracles, as well. A god of plenty, bringing food from the seas as well as the land, Dagon can be called on to bless feasts and food rituals.

Osiris—Death and Rebirth: This Egyptian god also takes care of the crops, the mind, the afterlife, and manners. Husband of Isis and father of Horus, Osiris is a green god who is deeply connected to the cycles of growing and changing seasons. Turn to him for rites of remembrance and for help with grief and mourning.

Buddha—Enlightenment and Wisdom: Although not a god, he is inspirational. He achieved enlightenment under the sacred Bodhi tree and passed on his knowledge to his followers.

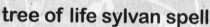

tree of life sylvan spell

This is a lovely spell to do if you are given a small tree as a gift, to wish for strength and good health for you and your love. Before you plant the sapling, tie a length of colored ribbon into a bow. Decorate the bow with a drawing of a heart or heart-shaped beads and place it in the hole you have dug for the tree. After planting the tree, water it well—especially with one or two tears of love, if possible! Make a wish that both you and your love will grow strong and enduring as the tree takes root and begins to flourish. When the tree bears its first leaf, press it in a book associated with the one you love. As long as you tend your tree with love, you will both enjoy blooming health and vitality.

Gods of inspiration and creativity

Apollo—*Friend to All Farmers:* Brother of the virgin goddess Artemis, Apollo is the god of music and the mind. If you are an artist, student, or musician, call on him for help with your creative pursuits. Writers can pray to him to banish writer's block and bring great success. Apollo is also the god of prophecy and truthfulness. According to ancient lore, he protected herds and flocks and is a friend to all farmers. Apollo and his son Asclepius also have dominion over medicine. Call on this god of light, sun, and healing when growing and mixing medicinal herbs.

Odin—*King of the Aesir:* The Norse equivalent of Zeus and Jupiter, Odin rules over wisdom, language, war, and poetry. You can appeal to him by carving runes or writing poetry. He can help you with any kind of writing, giving you the energy to forge ahead with purpose and passion. He can even help you to write your own rituals and poetic magical chants. Odin is associated with the celebrated Tree of Life.

Taliesin—*Monumental Figure:* Although not technically a god, Taliesin is said to live in the land of "summer stars," and is invoked in higher degrees of initiation in some esoteric orders. He is the poet of Welsh tradition, steeped in magic and mystery. He is associated with the magic of poetry, and embodies wisdom and clairvoyance. Taliesin is a helpmate to musicians and creative folks. If you are a solo practitioner and want to create a ceremony of self-initiation, Taliesin is a potent power to engage.

Hermes—*Kitchen Alchemy:* Hermes is associated with the Roman messenger god Mercury and the Egyptian scribe Thoth. Hermes is a key deity for astrologers and metaphysicians of every stripe, and is credited with the invention of alchemy. Kitchen witchery is nothing if not the alchemical magic of food and fire. Hermes is revered by ceremonial magicians and is believed to be the wisest of all. One of his domains is very important to cooks and ritualists: weights and measures.

Pan—*Playful Passion:* The goat god of the pastoral world oversees fields and forests, and therefore is connected to the earth. He is associated with love and lust, and is also good for music rites.

planting protection rite

According to Druids, the hazel is one of the nine sacred trees (the others are willow, alder, birch, ash, yew, elm, oak, and hawthorn). Hazel is a symbol of wisdom and sacred to the god of wisdom, Hermes. Working with hazelnuts or hazel wood can bring you deep knowledge, great luck, protection, and clairvoyance. You can bring fast luck to your home by stringing nine hazelnuts into a garland and hanging it over a door. For protection, tie hazel twigs into a bundle and hang it on the outside of your front door.

For psychic work, wearing a crown made of hazel twigs will intensify and deepen your divination practice. Speak this spell aloud:

Hermes' insight,

Hazel's grace and light,

Please come to me soon,

With tarot card, leaf of tea, or carved rune,

Lend me your wisdom under this sun and moon.

Everyday sacred A ritual guide to the days of the week

Each day of the week has specific correspondences and meanings. Here is an at-a-glance guide, gleaned from the mythologies of centuries past, to put into practice for different types of ritual. I do a money-enhancing ritual every Thursday, or "Thor's Day," which is the day for prosperity. Perhaps you want new love in your life; if so, try a "Freya's Day" ritual on a Friday night. Saturday is wonderful for charms and spells that bring a peaceful and happy home, including holding a dinner party at which you serve magical recipes and homemade liqueurs. Wednesday, ruled by Mercury and Virgo, is an excellent time for eco witchery homekeeping and gardening.

Sunday is the day for healing and vitality, as well as creativity and new hope. It is a day of confidence and success. This is the day that is ruled by the sun, so it corresponds to fire and to the sun sign, Leo. The colors for this day are gold, orange, and yellow, and the sacred stones are also in those colors: amber, citrine, carnelian, and topaz. Sunday's herbs and incense are cloves, cedar, chamomile, frankincense, amber, sunflower, and heliotrope.

Monday, or "Moon Day," is a dreamy day for intuition, beauty, women's rituals, and your home. Monday is associated with the element of water and the sign of Cancer. The colors are shiny silvers, pearl, pale rose, white, and lavender, which are reflective like the moon. The gems and stones are similar: moonstone, pearl, quartz crystal, fluorite, and aquamarine. The herbs and incense are night-blooming jasmine, myrtle, moonwort, vervain, white rose, poppy, and camphor.

Tuesday is the day for action, ruled by mighty Mars. Now you can seek your passion, surge toward your goals, find your destiny, and be strong and courageous. "Mars's Day" is the time for high energy in your career, for physical activity and sports, for aggression in meetings and negotiations, and for strong sexuality. Both fire and water come into play, and the astrological assignations are Aries and Scorpio. Red is the day's color, and the corresponding gems and crystals are ruby, garnet, carnelian, bloodstone, and pink tourmaline. Incense and herbs for Mars's Day are red roses, pine, carnation, nettle, patchouli, pepper, and garlic.

Wednesday, or "Odin's Day," is when the planets of communication, Mercury and Chiron, rule. This is the optimum time for writing, public speaking, intellectual pursuits, memory, and all other forms of communication. It is also a day to recognize your karmic duties through astrology and your Chiron sign, an important asteroid placement in your chart. Through introspection,

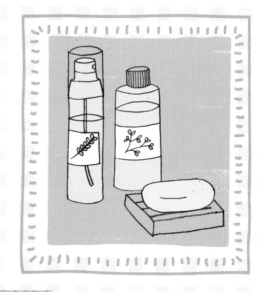

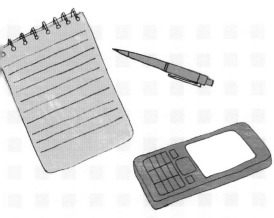

try to find your "sacred wound" and heal it so it does not hold you back in life, trapping you in old patterns and relationships. The element for Wednesday is earth and the sign is Virgo. Colors for this mercurial day are light blue, gray, green, orange, and yellow. The crystals are sodalite, moss agate, opal, and aventurine. The herbs and incense are cinnamon, periwinkle, dill, sweet pea, cinquefoil, and ferns.

Thursday is the day for business, politics, legal matters, bargaining, good fortune, and material and fiscal wealth. In other words, it is money day! The elements that come into play are water and fire, and Jupiter, the planet of abundance, is the ruler. Pisces and Sagittarius share this planet as ruler. The colors are blue, purple, and turquoise. As you might expect, the crystals are turquoise, sapphire, amethyst, and lapis lazuli, so favored by the Egyptians. The herbs and incense for the day are saffron, cedar, nutmeg, pine, oak, and cinnamon.

Friday is doubtless everybody's favorite day of the week, as it is ruled by Freya, the Nordic Venus, goddess of love. Friday is all about beauty, love, sex, fertility, friendships, and partnerships, the arts, harmony, and music, and bringing the new into your life—new energy, new people, new projects. Air and earth are the elements, and Libra and Taurus the astrological signs. Pale green and deep green, cyan blue, pink, and violet are the colors, and the crystals are emerald, pink tourmaline, rose quartz, jade, malachite, and peridot. The herbs and incense for Friday are apple, lily, birch, verbena, ivy, rose, and sage.

Saturday is ruled by Saturn and connects the elements of air, fire, water, and earth. It is a time for protection, discipline, duty, binding, family, manifestation, and completion. The signs are Capricorn and Aquarius, with their colors of black, brown, and deepest blue, and Saturday's crystals are amethyst, smoky quartz, jet, black onyx, obsidian, and darkest garnet. The incense, plants, and herbs for this day are ivy, oak, rue, moss, myrrh, deadly nightshade, mandrake, hemlock, and wolfsbane. (Many Saturn herbs are poisonous, so do exercise caution when using them.)

How do we use these magical correspondences in ritual? You can create your own ritual simply by choosing candle colors, crystals, and incense from the list that match your intent, and go from there.

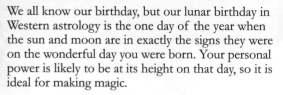

Moons of manifestation

Another factor in planning your rituals is the phases of the moon. You can fill your coffers and reduce the stress in your life by minding the moon. When it is waxing—growing from a new moon toward the full—this is a time to sow seeds and plant crops, a time for homekeeping and making spells to attract what you need. Use this time to bring the new into your life. When the moon is waning—gradually decreasing from a full moon back to a new moon—harvest crops, cut your hair, and shed anything you no longer want in your life. See the Resources section at the back of the book for help with keeping track of lunar phases, and note the results of your magical workings in your trusty Book of Shadows.

Your lunar birthday

We all know our birthday, but our lunar birthday in Western astrology is the one day of the year when the sun and moon are in exactly the signs they were on the wonderful day you were born. Your personal power is likely to be at its height on that day, so it is ideal for making magic.

You probably already know your sun sign (sometimes called your star sign), but perhaps not your moon sign, and you will also need to know what degree the moon was in at the time you were born. There are many websites that can help with this, but I recommend Cafe Astrology (see Resources on page 140).

To find out your lunar birthday, you then need to check the position of the planets and stars in an ephemeris for the current year. Again, I recommend Cafe Astrology for this. The ephemeris may look complicated, but you need only look at the first three columns, which show the day of the month, the position of the sun, and the position of the moon. You will see that at some point near your birthday, the sun and moon will be in the same signs as when you were born. There may be a few days of crossover, but the one that is your lunar birthday is when the sun and moon are in the same degree or close to it (this is the first number shown in the sun and moon columns). Each year will vary slightly, and sometimes it will line up with the actual date of your birth.

As an example, my psychic, Miguel, was born on September 17 with the sun in Virgo at 24° and the moon in Sagittarius at 9°. Let's work out his lunar birthday for 2018. By checking the ephemeris, I can see that the sun and moon are in the same signs as when he was born on September 15, 16, and 17; of those, the moon is closest to 9° on September 16 (when it is at 14°), meaning that in 2018 his lunar birthday is just a day before his solar birthday.

Happy lunar birthday spell

Make the most of this day of enchantment by writing down your birthday wishes, hopes, and dreams on a sheet of white paper. Light lots of incense and candles on your altar—every candle is your birthday candle today. Begin by invoking the lunar deities of your choice from the list on the right, and speak this spell:

I call upon the goddesses and gods of the moon, Astarte, Hathor, Luna, Soma, and Thoth (or change as appropriate).

On this day, my personal new year,

Grant me the grace and wisdom I need.

Grant me the soul and spirit I need.

Grant me the health and wealth I need.

Bring me the love and happiness I desire.

Make my home and family safe.

Now read out your list of hopes and dreams, then speak this prayer of gratitude to the deities:

I thank you for all of your wisdom and grace,

With harm to none, so mote it be!

Tie your list of wishes and dreams into a scroll using colored string, and place it on your altar. I leave my lunar birthday wish scroll on my home altar all year. I check it the following year, to see what came true, before tucking it into my Book of Shadows.

moon deities of the world

Call on any of these gods and goddesses, all of whom have an association with the moon within the religions and cultures that worship them, for your lunar magic:

- Aah
- Anahita
- Artemis
- Asherali
- Astarte
- Baiame
- Bendis
- Diana
- Gou
- Hathor
- Hecate
- Ilmaqah
- Ishtar
- Isis
- Jacy
- Khonsu
- Kilya
- Lucina
- Luna
- Mah
- Mama Quilla
- Mani
- Metztli
- Min
- Nanna
- Pah
- Selene
- Sin
- Soma
- Tsukuyomi
- Thoth
- Varuna
- Yarikh
- Yerak
- Zamna

Resources

Four Major Sabbats

Candlemas: February 2
Beltane: May 1
Lammas: August 1
Samhain: October 31

Four Lesser Sabbats

Vernal equinox: March 20
Summer solstice: June 24
Autumn equinox: September 23
Winter solstice/Yule:
December 21

Almanacs

THE OLD FARMER'S ALMANAC
almanac.com
For phases of the moon, sun and moon signs, gardening advice, recipes, and projects for home and garden (also available in print).

THE WITCHES' ALMANAC
thewitchesalmanac.com
For lunar lore, herbal lore, and astrological information.

Crystals, Oils, Herbs, and Other Supplies

CRYSTAL AGE
crystalage.com
For crystals, wands, crystalline statuary, and jewelry.

FOSSILERA
fossilera.com
For petrified wood and fossils.

JUNIPER TREE SUPPLIES
junipertreesupplies.com
For essential oils, carrier oils, soap, and candle-making supplies.

HERBS & ARTS
herbsandarts.com
For incense, burners, supplies, and herbs.

THE SCARLET SAGE HERB CO.
scarletsage.com
For dried herbs, essential oils, floral waters, and books.

TRADER JOE'S
traderjoes.com
For mini brooms.

Canning and Preserving

FRESH PRESERVING
freshpreserving.com/canning
To find stockists of supplies and jars, including Mason jars.

Gardening

SAVVY GARDENING
savvygardening.com
For gardening instructions and information on zones and climate.

GARDENER'S SUPPLY COMPANY
gardeners.com
For supplies.

GENERAL GARDENING RESOURCES
gardeningchannel.com/gardening
resources-best-gardening-sites
thegardeningwebsite.co.uk
rhs.org.uk

Astrology

CAFE ASTROLOGY
cafeastrology.com
Hugely useful site for all your astrology needs. Use the following links when working out your lunar birthday:

To find out your sun sign:
cafeastrology.com/whats-my-sun-sign.html

To find out your moon sign:
cafeastrology.com/whats-my-moon-sign.html

To find the ephemeris for previous and upcoming years to determine your lunar birthday:
cafeastrology.com/
ephemeris.html

Index

A

almanacs 140
almond oil 55, 75
almonds 101
altar
    consecrating 31
    fireplace 33
    house magic 30–2
    natural 34–5
aphrodisiacs 76–7, 112, 113, 116
apple brandy spirits 108
apricots 112
Aquarius 91, 111
Aries 90, 111
aromatherapy see essential oils
astrological resources 140
astrological signs 90–1, 111
avocado 112

B

baking soda 43, 52, 54, 56
banana 113
basil 88, 116
basil oil 92
bath time
    body whip 58
    coconut milk bath 79
    gratitude chant 60
    oatmeal soother 55
    purification soak 61
    sandalwood salts 78
bathroom 28, 45
beans, green 84, 121
bedroom
    bed blessing 72
    charm/spell box 29
    self-care spell 72
    setting the mood 70–1, 73
beets/beetroot 83, 94, 121
birds, significance 87
blackberries 114, 118
blessings, gratitude for 32, 49,
    60
blueberries 114

body blessing 59
body lotion 55, 57
body scrubs 52–3
body whip 58
bolline, sanctifying 33
Book of Shadows 17, 28, 29, 74,
    111, 113
box, magical 29
bread, cheesy beer 98
brooms 11

C

cabbage, coleslaw 100
Cancer 90, 111
candles 27, 30, 71, 72, 74
canning 91, 107, 140
Capricorn 91, 111
carrots 82, 96, 99, 100
celery 121
chakras, crystal healing 64–7
changes, making 6, 49
cheese grater, cleaning 44
cherry 112
chives 88
cleaners, organic 37–49
    all-purpose 38–9
    baking soda 43, 52
    consecrating 48
    floor 39
    laundry detergent 42
    lemons 44–5
    salt 43
    scrub 41
    self-care 51
    shelf life 42, 52
    stain removal 43
    tea tree wipes 42
    vinegar 42
    yogurt polish 43
clearing space 11
clocks, striking 78
clutter
    in bedroom 70, 71
    decluttering 9–17

psychic 12–13
coconut
    magical correspondence 101
    milk bath 79
    oil 55, 58
coffee scrub 53
coleslaw 100
color, significance 47
compost, tea from 84
copper, yogurt polish 43
coriander 88
corn, baked pudding 95
courgettes, properties 121
creation, goddesses of 128–9
creativity, gods of 134
crystals see gems and crystals
cucumbers, pickled 120–1
cutting board, cleaning 44

D

days of the week 136–7
decluttering 9–17
dining room, candles 27
doorways, herbal wreaths 25
dreams, prophecy incense 32

E

energy
    bad 12–13, 18, 21, 114
    cleansing 22, 24
    maintenance 18, 20, 48–9
entrance/porch 10, 24–5
essential oils
    carrier oils 75
    energy maintenance 20
    romance and rest 73, 74–9

F

facial products 54, 57
feng shui 18–19, 61, 70–1
fig 114
fireplace altar 33
floors 11, 39–41, 44
flower essences 105–7

Acknowledgments

I am deeply grateful to publisher Cindy Richards and CICO Books for the honor of working together. I can honestly say I have never seen a publishing house lavish more care on their books. This is a great rarity these days, and the attention to detail shows on every lovely page. The books are simply gorgeous and I am proud of my books published by CICO, which I consider to be works of art. Rosie Scott's illustrations brought my ideas to life, while art director Sally Powell manages the art and design with grace and élan. Designer Mark Latter's layout is truly inspired, and copy editor Rosie Fairhead's work made my words a pleasure to read. Kerry Lewis and Eliana Holder are incredibly helpful in bringing all the pieces together, and big thanks to Mai-Ling Collyer, who makes sure the finished books are things of beauty. And they are.

None of this could happen without the wise guidance of Carmel Edmonds and Kristine Pidkameny. I am in such good hands with these two wonder women. Carmel made sense of my writing when occasionally I didn't and everything she touches is improved upon. Kristine, my friend of many years, is a goddess of discernment and my guide throughout the process. Thanks to these two, my books are truly filled with magic. Thanks to all of you for an enchanted experience for this writer.

Bright blessings!

THE
FAIRY GODMOTHER'S
GROWTH GUIDE